About
the
Author

Edward Margolies is a professor of
English and American Studies at the
College of Staten Island of the City
University of New York. He received
his B.A. from Brown University and
his M.A. and Ph.D. from New York
University. Professor Margolies was
Senior Fulbright Lecturer at the Uni-
versity of Nijmegen, Holland, in 1977
and Visiting Professor of American
Studies at the University of Paris (III),
France, in 1979. He is the author of *Na-
tive Sons—A Critical Study of Twen-
tieth Century Negro American Authors*
(Lippincott, 1968), *The Art of Richard
Wright* (Southern Illinois University
Press, 1969), *A Native Sons Reader*
(Editor, Lippincott, 1970). *Afro-Ameri-
can Fiction, 1853—1976* (co-author,
Gale Research Co., 1979), and many
articles on American literature. Margolies lives in New York City.

Which Way Did He Go?

Which Way Did He Go?

THE PRIVATE EYE IN DASHIELL HAMMETT RAYMOND CHANDLER, CHESTER HIMES, AND ROSS MACDONALD

EDWARD MARGOLIES

HM
Essay and General Literature Index
HOLMES & MEIER PUBLISHERS, Inc.
NEW YORK • LONDON

First published in the United States of America 1982 by
Holmes & Meier Publishers, Inc.
30 Irving Place, New York, N.Y. 10003

Holmes & Meier Publishers Ltd.
131 Trafalgar Road
Greenwich, London SE109TX

Library of Congress Cataloging in Publication Data

Margolies, Edward
   Which way did he go?

  Bibliography: p.
  Includes index.
    1. Detective and mystery stories, American—
History and criticism.   2. Heroes in literature.
I. Title.
PS374.D4M3 1981   813'.0872'09352   81-1061
AACR2

ISBN 0-8419-0436-7   ISBN 0-8419-0790-0 (paper)

Manufactured in the United States of America

For Claire

Contents

Sources and Acknowledgments

It is impossible to account for all of one's debts. Years of reading and discussions with others about the ideas in this book are not easy to track down. First off, then, my apologies for unacknowledged sources. But I am sure, too, that some of the views I express here diverge considerably from those of the publications and persons I especially wish to acknowledge. Clearly, they are not responsible for what I have written; I wish only to say that I found their works helpful, informative, and stimulating.

What follows then are the names of several of the publications I consulted for bibliographies, literary history, and background material on the lives of the authors and for cultural and critical assessments. For reasons of space I have omitted very nearly all the pieces I have read in journals. Most of these, however, are listed in the bibliographies and collections I cite.

Two recent indispensable bibliographies of crime and detective fiction are Allen J. Hubin's *The Bibliography of Crime Fiction, 1749–1975* (Del Mar, Ca.: Publishers Inc., 1979) and John M. Reilly's *Twentieth-Century Crime and Mystery Writers* (New York: St. Martin's Press, 1980). Other important bibliographic material may be found in Jacques Barzun and Wendell Hertig Taylor's *A Catalogue of Crime* (New York: Harper & Row, 1971); Ordean Hagen's *Who Done It? A Guide to Mystery and Suspense Fiction* (New York: R. R. Bowker, 1969); Chris Steinbrunner et al, *Encyclopedia of Mystery and Detection* (New York: McGraw Hill, 1976) and James Sandoe's checklist, "The Private Eye" in *The Mystery Story*, edited by John Ball (New York: Penguin Books, 1978).

There are also important periodicals containing up-to-date bibliographies, reviews, and essays on tough-guy detective fiction. Two of the best are *The Armchair Detective,* and *Ellery Queen's Mystery Magazine.*

For an overall history and assessment of detective fiction, I liked best Julian Symon's *Mortal Consequences* (New York: Harper & Row, 1972). William Ruehlmann writes principally about hardboiled private eyes, and although I did not agree with his thesis, I found much that was useful in his text and bibliography (*Saint With a Gun,* New York: New York University Press, 1974).

There are several good collections of essays on crime and detective fiction, some of which deal with the hardboiled genre. Among them are Howard Haycraft's *The Art of the Mystery Story* (New York: Simon & Schuster, 1946), Francis M. Nevins Jr., *The Mystery Writer's Art* (Bowling Green, Ohio: Popular Press, 1970), and Larry N. Landrum et al, *Dimensions of Detective Fiction* (Popular Press, 1976). David Madden edited an excellent collection of essays, *Tough Guy Writers of the Thirties* (Carbondale: Southern Illinois University Press, 1968), all of which pertain to the subject matter in this book. In addition I profited from reading unpublished doctoral dissertations on private eye fiction by Alan B. Crider (University of Texas, 1973) and Robert B. Parker (Boston University, 1971).

There are three anthologies whose introductions recount the pulp origins of tough-guy dicks: *The Hard-Boiled Omnibus,* edited by Joseph T. Shaw (New York, Simon & Schuster, 1946); *The Hardboiled Dicks,* edited by Ron Goulart (New York: Pocket Books, 1967), and *Stories From Black Mask Magazine, 1920–51,* edited by Herbert Ruhm (New York: Vintage Books, 1977).

Despite some factual errors, Russel Nye's *The Unembarrassed Muse* (New York: Dial, 1970) remains the best overall survey of American popular culture. Two full-length accounts of popular literature are James D. Hart's *The Popular Book: A History of America's Literary Taste* (Berkeley and Los Angeles: University of California Press, 1963) and Frank Luther Mott's *Golden Multitudes: The Story of Best Sellers in the United States* (New York: R. R. Bowker, 1947). Chapters in Henry Nash Smith's *Virgin Land: The American West as Symbol and Myth* (Cambridge: Harvard University Press, 1950) deal with heroics in dime novels and other kinds of popular fiction. A first-rate analysis of the hero in high culture may be found in Theodore L. Gross's *The Heroic Ideal in American Literature* (New York: The Free Press, 1971). For more specialized material on popular publications, see Mary Noel's *Villains Galore: The Heyday of the Popular Story Weekly* (New York: Macmillan, 1954), Albert Johannsen's *The House of Beadle and Adams and its dime and nickel novels: The Story of a Vanished Literature* (Norman, Okla.: University of Oklahoma Press, 1950); Frank Gruber's *The Pulp Jungle* (Los Angeles: Sherbourne Press, 1967) and Harold Brainerd Hersey's *Pulpwood Editor* (New York: Frederick A. Stokes, 1937).

I found very provocative ideas about the psychological and cultural functions of city literature in Raymond Williams's *The Country and the City* (London: Chatto and Windus Ltd., 1973). Among other suggestive works are John C. Cawelti's exploration of popular aesthetics in *The Six Gun Mystique* (Bowling Green, Ohio: Popular Press, 1971) and *Adventures, Mystery and Romance* (Chicago: University of Chicago Press, 1976), and Richard Slotkin's treatment of violence as a theme in early American writing in *Regeneration through Violence* (Middletown, Conn.: Wesleyan University Press, 1973). Several of Leslie A. Fiedler's works deal with eros and thanatos; one of these, *The Return of the Vanishing Indian* (New York: Stein and Day, 1968), focuses on violent females.

At present, Richard Layman's *Shadow Man: The Life of Dashell Hammett* (New York: Harcourt Brace Jovanovich/Bruccoli Clark, 1981) is the only full-length biography of Dashiell Hammett, although at least one other is being prepared. Much of what I wrote about Hammett's life I drew from Lillian Hellman's memoirs, *An Unfinished Woman* (Boston: Little Brown, 1969) and *Pentimento* (Little Brown, 1973), and most of this material may be found in her introduction to a recent collection of Hammett's stories, *The Big Knockover* (New York: Vintage Books, 1972). There are brief biographical allusions in Steven Marcus's very perceptive introduction to another collection of Hammett's stories, *The Continental Op* (New York: Vintage Books, 1974) and a somewhat longer account of Hammett's life in William F. Nolan's *Dashiell Hammett: A Casebook* (Santa Barbara, Ca.: McNally & Loftin, 1969). *The City of San Francisco Magazine*, Nov. 4, 1975, published interviews with Hammett's first wife and Pinkerton detectives who knew him as a colleague. The most exhaustive and scholarly bibliography is Richard Layman's *Dashiell Hammett: A Descriptive Bibliography* (Pittsburgh: University of Pittsburgh Press, 1979).

To date there are two biographies of Raymond Chandler: Philip Durham's *Down These Mean Streets a Man Must Go: Raymond Chandler's Knight* (Chapel Hill: University of North Carolina Press, 1963) and Frank MacShane's much more extensive, *The Life of Raymond Chandler* (New York: E. P. Dutton, 1976). Some of Chandler's friends reminisce about him in *The World of Raymond Chandler*, edited by Miriam Gross (New York: A. & W. Publishers, 1978). See also *The Notebooks of Raymond Chandler*, edited by Frank MacShane (New York: Ecco Press, 1978). A number of Chandler's letters are reproduced in *Raymond Chandler Speaking,* edited by Dorothy Gardiner and Kathrine Sorley Walker (Boston: Houghton Mifflin, 1977). For other correspondence see *Letters, Raymond Chandler and James Fox*, edited by James Pepper (Santa Barbara, Ca.: Neville and Yellin, 1979). Although a great deal has been written about Chandler, I found Leon Howard's "Raymond Chandler's Not-So-Great Gatsby" in *The Mystery and Detection Annual* (Beverly Hills, Ca.: 1973), revealing not only about Chandler but, by extension, other hardboiled writers as well. Bibliographical listings may be found in Matthew J. Bruccoli's books: *Raymond Chandler: A Checklist* (Kent, Oh.: Kent State University Press, 1968); *Chandler Before Marlowe: Raymond Chandler's Early Prose and Poetry, 1908–1912* (Columbia, S.C.: University of South Carolina Press, 1973), as well as in Bruccoli's latest book, *Raymond Chandler: A Descriptive Bibliography* (Pittsburgh: University of Pittsburgh Press, 1979).

Chester Himes's two volumes of autobiography constitute most of the published material about his life: *The Quality of Hurt* (Garden City, N.Y.: Doubleday, 1972), and *My Life of Absurdity* (Doubleday, 1976). The latter deals in part with his crime novels. Other biographical and critical pieces about Himes are listed in Stephen F. Milliken's bibliography in *Chester Himes: A*

Critical Appraisal (Columbia, Mo.: University of Missouri Press, 1976). Additional Himes bibliographies and checklists are cited in Edward Margolies and David Bakish, *Afro-American Fiction, 1853–1976: A Guide To Information Sources* (Detroit: Gale Research Company, 1979).

Ross Macdonald writes a great deal about himself in the forewords to three of his novels collected in *Archer in Hollywood* (New York: Alfred A. Knopf, 1967) and three others collected in *Archer At Large* (Knopf, 1970). See also two autobiographical essays, *On Crime Writing* (Santa Barbara, Ca.: Capra Press, 1973) and his autobiographical introduction to *Lew Archer, Private Investigator* (Yonkers, N.Y.: Mysterious Press, 1977). Two books about his work are Peter Wolfe's *Dreamers Who Live Their Dreams: The World of Ross Macdonald's Novels* (Bowling Green, Oh.: Popular Press, 1976) and a short survey, Jerry Speir's *Ross Macdonald* (New York: Ungar, 1980). For bibliographical material, interviews, and another Macdonald autobiographical introduction see Matthew J. Bruccoli's *Kenneth Millar/Ross Macdonald, A Checklist* (Detroit: Gale Research Company, 1971).

In addition to acknowledging a debt to the above sources, I want to express thanks to John M. Reilly for sending me material he has written on tough-guy letters. I also want to thank Doris Alexander and Bart Midwood who read portions of this manuscript and made valuable suggestions. Finally, I should like to acknowledge the contribution of my colleague, Richard Gid Powers whose views on popular culture I found often unusual and always provocative.

Which Way Did He Go?

CHAPTER 1

Introduction

This book is about heroes. Tough, hardboiled, individualistic, cynical, sometimes sneering, and always courageous. They belong to America's popular literature, emerging some time after World War I and flourishing throughout World War II. After World War II, some of them tried, not very convincingly, to hold onto their old ways, some of them modified their behavior, and some of them went beserk with violence and rage at the changed conditions of life.

The chapters that follow focus on the heroes of four authors—Dashiell Hammett, Raymond Chandler, Chester Himes, and Ross Macdonald—who reveal and typify many of the underlying principles of popular fiction and who are, I believe, representative of shifting social and cultural attitudes.

The usual detective hero belongs to the world of popular culture as opposed to the world of high art. He is largely a creature of the mass media who nourishes the daydreams of his readers. But this in itself does not separate him from the realm of high art.

High art, in form or content, subverts ordinary perceptions of reality and hints at alternate interpretations of experience. Popular culture, on the other hand, tends to reinforce one's private fantasies and yet to reconfirm social and moral attitudes as well. Thus popular culture succeeds by producing an uneasy competition between an individual's unconscious wishes and the public's sense of acceptable values. For example, a love story written for a slick magazine in the 1930s might deal with a young woman's resistance to the sexual allure of an older or wealthy or married man. Her self-discipline, we are told, is justified because soon a virile, younger fellow will come along and ask for her hand. Clearly, the demands of the libido and society are in conflict in our hypothetical but not untypical story, and popular culture usually comes down hard on the side of society. But what the story also implies is that the heroine's physical needs will be better satisfied after marriage.

To take another example, in the traditional western, we are sometimes asked to believe that it was necessary to tame unruly nature and anarchic outlaws in order to advance American democracy and civilization. But the heroes of western sagas often indulge their own lawless, anarchic impulses in order to gain these ends. Hence the reader has his law-and-order cake and eats it too. Something like this also happens in tough detective stories, where heroes ruthlessly break the law in order to attain justice. But as we shall see, a few authors employing popular forms have escaped the usual conservative conclusions. Their works constitute a grey area lying somewhere between high art and popular writing. The effectiveness of elitist fiction is measured by its ability to surprise or communicate a fresh, original, or unusual understanding of experience to an audience. The effectiveness of a popular writer, on the other hand, lies chiefly in the way that he conceals from his reader something that the reader already knows or secretly believes. This knowledge may include ideas that are politically and socially acceptable—if not government sanctioned— for example, that the winning of the American West was a good thing. But sometimes the outlook contained in a work of popular culture may be at odds with official views, as for example when outlaws or Indians become heroes or premarital or extramarital sex is regarded as desirable. When this happens the study of popular culture may reveal serious underground rifts in the society at large.

Popular writing, almost by definition, implies predetermined plot structures, character types, and stylistic techniques that are here considered under the broad rubric of formula. There are formulas for war stories and popular romance as well as formulas for detective fiction. These will vary from one period to the next as historical circumstance and social attitudes change. But, as a rule, such change is slow, giving works in the popular culture a remarkable consistency. In a famous 1930s play parodying Hollywood, a couple of prospective screen writers are told that however they write their love stories, they must write them in the following manner: boy meets girl, boy loses girl, boy gets girl. The successful popular writer may, within limits, seek variations and it is part of his skill not to make the formula too obvious, but there exists nonetheless a tacit agreement between author and audience that the former stick to fundamentals. Audiences may not be able to articulate explicitly what the formula is, but they know what they want and demand it as their right.

The popular hardboiled detective story is composed of a number of basic, formulaic elements. Essentially it describes the detective's recruitment for a dangerous assignment, carnal and material rewards if he drops the case, "ritual" beatings and threats to his life if he does not, and his persistence and courage in carrying on despite these diversions. The detective is himself often a "type"—a bachelor, individualistic, unswervingly honest, isolated and classless, who tends to regard most social and political institutions as soft or too amenable to corruption. The hardboiled genre is a peculiar mix, celebrating American individualism while at the same time denigrating the corruption of American society. As nearly every reader of hardboiled fiction knows, even the style in these stories is formulaic, with the adventure usually related in the first person by the detective himself who, when not given to tortured similes, is usually terse, laconic and objective, simply telling what he sees, hears, thinks, and feels.

The writers selected for this study are thematically ambivalent about social and cultural values, but what makes them especially interesting is that due perhaps to the peculiarities of their temperaments, the "rules" of popular literature may in some ways have actually freed their imagination. This is not so odd as it may at first appear. One thinks of Renaissance popes or princes ordering standardized Biblical and classical themes from painters whose works may have benefited as much by these commands as by their absence. Within certain limitations they were free to indulge their creativity and were liberated at least from the anxiety of seeking their subjects. Whatever the compromises they made in their private lives, no one today thinks of the old masters as having compromised their vision; the imposition of formulas need not destroy individuality or artistic power. Possibly none of the writers treated in this study belongs comfortably among the ranks of high artists, nor even fully succeeded in exploiting the possibilities of the medium. But this may have less to do with deficiencies of their talents than with the changing social, historical, and psychological conditions that produced the genre. A glance backwards at some of the strands that helped contribute to the hardboiled detective story may well be in order. Some of these strands are woven out of the social fiber of early twentieth-century America.

In an essay called "The Way Out" (*Tough Guy Writers of the Thirties,* edited by David Madden, Southern Illinois University Press, 1968), Kingsley Widmer asserts that the tough-guy ethos was somehow also embedded in the real-life subculture of the American hobo. As evidence, Widmer points to the memoirs of former hoboes that celebrate the violent marginal lives of men on the open road. Several of these accounts were written around the first decade of the new century (Jack London's *The Road,* 1910, being a good example), often by men who had become successful authors and journalists. They speak nostalgically of their male group past as if they had lost a certain purity. Their attitudes linger on, says Widmer, in novels like Jack Kerouac's *On The Road* and Clancy Sigal's *Going Away.*

When the last years of the nineteenth century drew to a close, being tough was sometimes more a necessity than a virtue. Seemingly arbitrary business and agricultural cycles displaced from the land growing numbers of young men who hopped on passing freights or tramped the open roads, taking odd jobs wherever they could find them. Soon they were joined by similarly dispossessed city dwellers who, in addition, resented the impersonalization of urban industrial life. Their existence was not easy, as they often had to face the wrath of police as well as outraged citizens of respectable communities, who regarded all vagrants as undesirable. As a reaction, hoboes developed a kind of ethos that valued toughness and courage as virtues and celebrated hard drink and physical violence as a means of proving worth. The hoboes extolled what they said was their freedom and displayed open contempt for middle-class regimentation. Life, they declared, was hostile or, at best, devoid of purpose. Bravery, they believed, was facing these facts squarely. "God is guts," quotes Widmer, from an early hobo song. Clearly, hardboiled detectives owed something to the spirit of these men.

More immediately, tough detective fiction gleaned some of its inspiration from post-World War I headlines. Violent crimes, especially open warfare among competing bootlegging gangs, drew constant media attention. Americans who felt themselves lost in the shuffle of mass society discovered that they were not altogether out of sympathy with the lawbreakers. For whoever else they were, gangsters rose from the invisible lower orders and realized American dreams of success, individual identity, and power. If their pride and fame foreshadowed inevitable defeat, their lives somehow acquired a kind of tragic aura. The gangster hero of F. Scott Fitzgerald's *The Great Gatsby* (1925) would later capitalize on this image of the outsider as tragic hero. We shall observe in forthcoming chapters how Fitzgerald's novel influenced the works of several writers of hardboiled detective fiction. In their way, of course, pulp writers were only responding to fashionable post-war attitudes, but in a deeper sense they were also expressing a widespread disillusionment with twenty years of progressive reform whose chief fruits appeared to be unworkable Prohibition laws and the broken promises of World War I. Expatriate writers like Ernest Hemingway (*The Sun Also Rises* and *A Farewell to Arms*) recorded similar attitudes among Americans abroad. Writers as disparate as Hammett and Hemingway shared the desire to start over, to communicate only what was known, felt, or seen, stripped of the "lies," the illusions or the self-deceptions of the past. Their terse, tense style (short sentences, short paragraphs, earthy simple concrete Anglo Saxon words and an absence of abstract and judgmental adjectives) bespeaks a cautious outlook as much as anything they say. The tough noncommital pose of their heroes tells us that they may have been hurt once, believed once, but no more—that they cannot, will not, be taken in again. Of one thing they were certain—that life was violent. To ask, as some critics do, whether high art influenced popular art or vice versa is fruitless. Both responded to their times. Between the two, they produced a kind of prose that would influence another generation of writers.

Other strands in the development of detective fiction are more purely literary in nature. Perhaps we should begin by saying that the detective story is one of the most "American" of literary forms. Most of what passes now as "traditional" detective fiction follows the pattern set down in Edgar Allan Poe's three short stories about the Parisian detective, Monsieur Dupin. A puzzle or problem that baffles the authorities is brought to the master detective and Dupin undertakes to solve the problem chiefly by exercising his immense intellect. If Dupin were to tell these stories himself, he would have to let the reader in on his thought processes, so the tales are related by an admiring companion who, although possessing the same information as the master detective, obviously does not possess his powers of deduction. A direct line may be drawn from Poe's Dupin through Arthur Conan Doyle's Sherlock

Holmes to Rex Stout's Nero Wolfe, all of whom apprehend criminals by using their intellect rather than violence, although they may on occasion bestir themselves. By and large these detectives are gentlemen who rarely question the social conditions that produce criminals. They not only defend the status quo but, more important, they *believe* in the status quo. One feels that once they have identified the perpetrators of crime, all will be well with their worlds.

Although they are a much later breed and do, indeed, feel unhappy about social inequalities the 1920s hardboiled-action school of authors also derives from Poe. First, the puzzle element of crime fiction—although it exists to a much lesser degree—is not altogether absent; it is often the excuse for the detective's adventures and demands some resolution. Second, there is still disrespect for official authority in solving crimes, and a concomitant faith in the superior individual who not only defies the police but beats them at their own game. Third, there is the assertion of the detective's will and the element of his lawlessness. By a supreme effort of his will, the ratiocinative detective, as Poe would call him, breaks down doors, intrudes on the privacy of people, and even assaults them, *but only in his mind*. What that genteel detective did intellectually, the hardboiled-action detective will have to do physically, transmuting violent fantasies into reality. Finally, the contemporary hero resembles his gentler ancestor in that both are lonely isolated figures who brood about a world replete with terror, menace, and death and both, in order to withstand an engulfing sense of horror, manage to anesthetize their feelings. The price of survival for the individual who constantly confronts crime, it seems, is emotional atrophy.

If one literary strand of the hardboiled genre extends to Poe, another reaches back to the western or frontier adventure tale. The western and the detective genres begin to merge in the 1870s at a time when America's frontiers were contracting rapidly and new and booming industrial cities were beginning to appear. The setting for most detective fiction is, of course, the city, but the generic distinctions between popular detective fiction and the popular western are not all that pronounced. In fact, from the start, many authors created both kinds, and even Dashiell Hammett, one of the founding fathers of the hardboiled school, wrote westerns for pulp magazines early in his career. After Hammett, lesser authors of detective stories in the 1930s and 1940s freely exchanged "specialized" data with one another in order to write other kinds of fiction—sea stories, World War I stories, or whatever else the market demanded, including westerns; regardless of the type of adventure stories they produced, certain western-formulaic components remained fairly constant. Nor do western and detective fiction linkages end there. In the post-World War II period, Ross Macdonald's hero, Lew Archer, alludes to himself in more than one book as a descendant of James Fenimore Cooper's Leatherstocking frontiersmen. Today, the action detectives' fiercest competition may be found among the heroes of the science fiction genre, but even here a case could be made that science fiction tales are still only westerns under their futuristic skin.

Archer's implicit acknowledgment of the tough-guy detective's frontier ancestry is not out of line with what a number of scholars of American culture had already observed. With fewer and fewer animals to hunt and rustlers and Indians to shoot, the western hero turned to the city to pursue other prey. No longer a lone ranger of sorts, he became a private eye—still outside organized society, but curiously trapped inside as well. As a cowboy or a hunter he had shunned towns and cities because they were too crowded and corrupt and curbed his freedom. As a hunter and a frontiersman he broke trail for hordes of settlers and farmers, however much he despised them, but as a private detective he is doomed to live among the people he saves. If the frontiersman conquered the West in the name of the civilization from which he fled, the private eye overcomes his enemies for a kind of justice he believes his society is incapable of rendering. With no West to which he could escape, he falls back upon himself and becomes cynical and near-paranoid.

The detective's ambivalence toward women may also be traced to the frontiersmen, who tended to identify women with organized social institutions such as family, church, the schools, and the arts. In their flight from society, the frontiersmen fled women who would imprison them in a tainted polity and dampen their idealism with the pragmatic demands of a domestic life. Natty Bumppo and Huck Finn are but two of a host of American literary heroes who move west to get away from women and civilization. The tough private eye loves and hates women because, being confined to cities, he cannot avoid their presence. There are, to be sure, damsels in distress that the detective as knight errant must protect; they are everywhere in Chandler and exist to a lesser degree in Hammett and Macdonald. On the other hand, the most treacherous deceivers, criminals, and corrupters are also often women, and one of the measures of the tough guy's toughness is his ability to cope with women as handily as he copes with men. The ardor with which he sometimes undertakes this task betrays the violence of his emotions.

> He took one cat-like step toward her and hit her. His fist didn't travel more than six inches, and it landed with a sharp smack on the hinge of her jaw just below the ear. Teresa Mayan whirled around with a graceful rustle of silk, fell across the divan and rolled off on the floor. She lay motionless, face down. . . . 'This isn't going to hurt me more than it does you,' Latin told her conversationally. 'In fact, I just love to bat people around. You tell me where that film is or you're going to be in the market for store teeth.' ["Don't Give Your Right Name" by Norbert Davis in *Dime Detective,* December 1941]

One need not look only to popular culture for hostile attitudes toward women; Washington Irving's Rip Van Winkle's rather lengthy departure from both his village and his shrewish wife is surely illustrative of our point. But in Cooper's and Irving's works, misogyny and escape do not necessarily imply violence toward women. This would have to await the advent of tough-guy detective fiction in the 1920s.

There was, however, violence aplenty in the western, directed toward

Indians, toward uncurbed nature (forests and buffalo, say) and, oddly enough, toward the heroes of these works themselves. The protagonists of popular writing are often required to undergo baptisms of fire in order to prove their mettle. The ritual beating received by the hardboiled detective is really no more than an extension of this literary convention. In order to fully understand the phenomenon, however, it may be necessary to return to an even earlier tradition, beginning with the late seventeenth-century captivity narratives. Nearly five hundred different titles of this genre have been collected. By and large, they purport to be true accounts of the adventures of white settlers who had been captured by merciless Indians. They are also, in their way, escape narratives, like many of the immensely popular slave narratives published in the 1840s and 1850s, but unlike the latter, escape sometimes involved committing mayhem on one's captors. One famous eighteenth century escapee, a Haverhill Massachusetts woman named Hannah Duston, tells of hacking off the heads of her sleeping Indian captors. This gory event made her a heroine and her story was retold many times. Paradoxically, the theme of escape in captivity writings suggests a symbolic evasion of Christian civilizing restraints in order to regain entry into Christian society. In effect, the libido pretends it is the superego. Violent passions are indulged, in the name of safeguarding religion and community.

Thus from the start not only were America's first best-sellers violent, but they featured violent heroes and heroines. The violence they commit and the beatings and torture inflicted on them were perceived as a means of testing their Christian faith. In nearly all the early narratives, the captives speak of their gratitude to the Deity who alone is responsible for their survival under cruel circumstances. But if they had their God to thank for their deliverance, He dealt with them as individuals and not through social institutions or religious intermediaries. And they, in turn, regarded themselves as extensions of His will, wreaking vengeance and death on their enemies—which may be another source of the arbitrary righteousness and lawless behavior of their nineteenth- and twentieth-century descendants in popular literature. The violent acts inflicted upon them—the scalpings, tortures, and torments these first heroes suffered at the hands of their enemies—are not unlike the ritual beatings private eyes would take when they were captured by gangsters or hostile policemen. In either instance, early and late, heroes come perilously close to death. Their triumph is their survival.

One of the earliest popular adventure fiction writers was Sylvanus Cobb, Jr. who in more than thirty years wrote nearly three thousand pieces of varying lengths. These first appeared in the late 1840s in what were then being called "story papers"—weekly newspapers whose chief attraction was serialized fiction. Initially sold through the mails at subscription rates, the "story papers" later established themselves as standard items on newsstands. Cobb's heroes were constantly being subjected to violence; at the time of his death, one of his readers wrote an elegy to their endurance:

Sylvanus took his hero where a hero ought to go,
In scrapes an' awful dangers where he seemed to have no show;
He drowned him, shot him, scalped him, but every reader knew
Sylvanus knew his business well and he would pull him through.
He bruised him, banged him, buried him, an' did a han'some job,
But still we knew the chap was safe with ol' Sylvanus Cobb.
[Quoted in James D. Hart, *The Popular Book*, 1950]

Not all Cobb's heroes were westerners (his most famous work was called "The Gunmakers of Moscow"), but they all embraced frontier heroics; the protagonists were extreme individualists, depending mainly on their own courage, brawn, skills, and luck for survival, and they were all killers of one sort or another.

The kind of western hero most familiar to present-day audiences began appearing in the yellow paper-covered, mass-produced dime novels of the new publishing house of Beadle and Adams in 1860. These books, exceedingly popular among Union soldiers during the Civil War, were soon imitated by other publishers jealous of their success. Chief among Beadle and Adams's competitors for the next thirty or more years would be George Munro, Robert de Will, Frank Munro, Frank Tousey, and Street and Smith, each of which distributed books in the hundreds of thousands. Many of these dime novels dealt with nonwestern subject matter ranging from foreign intrigue to love stories, but westerns and, by the 1880s, detective mysteries, drew the greatest number of readers.

Much of the material of dime novels was turned out by hacks, who were, at the same time, producing similar kinds of fiction for the story papers. They assumed a variety of pseudonyms and would, on occasion, write books on a sort of production line, one author doing one chapter, a second another, and so on until the novel was deemed complete. Although the heroes they created were aristocrats in their fashion, they were all democratically conceived; they were often of humble origin, but performed as impeccably as any knight, especially when rescuing beautiful maidens from lusting red savages. Such rescues were always fraught with dangers, as were the heroes' other activities. "Twenty deaths per novel was not unusual," writes Russel Nye in *The Unembarrassed Muse,* and the formula always demanded at least one dangerous crisis per chapter. As might be expected, style and dialogue were often as histrionic and implausible as the plots. Here is an excerpt from a Buffalo Bill story:

Can the memory of my good father, butchered in cold blood before his poor wife and helpless children, ever pass away? No, Bill, never, never! I will never feel that he rested easy in his grave while one of them is alive to boast of the darkest deed he has done. I have with my own hand killed two-thirds of them, and until all are gone—and by my hand too, I will not feel content. I heard the wretch groaning from pain this morning. It was music to my soul. [Quoted in Mary Noel, *Villains Galore,* 1954]

However removed these tales seem today from tough, terse, hardboiled detective fiction, they foreshadow not only the chivalric, knight-errant quality of their heroes but also, unfortunately, their racism; in one of the first dime novel best-sellers, *Malaeska, or the Indian Wife of the White Hunter* (1860), the son of the union of the two races commits suicide when he learns he is a half breed.

Nor was all violence in their stories confined to men. In the 1870s a number of dime novels began featuring white heroines who dress as men and who were as adept as their male counterparts in cutting down villains and Indians. They had learned their killing ways as one-time captives of Indians, and were now exercising their arts effectively. The sexual identity of these fictional descendants of Hannah Duston may have caused some uneasiness but there can be little doubt that they were popular with readers. In their fashion they were the precursors of tough killer females in the writings of 1920s authors.

Although nearly all western heroes were fictional, a few early dime novels began portraying historical characters like Kit Carson, Davy Crockett, or Daniel Boone, whose killing of "b'ars" was by now legend. In 1869, an adventurer and sometime publisher, Edward Zane Caroll Judson, better known as Ned Buntline, fictionalized the life of an obscure Army scout named William Cody, thereby beginning a burgeoning Buffalo Bill industry. More-over, by the 1870s, several real-life outlaws also made fictionalized ap-pearances, among them Frank and Jesse James, Billy the Kid, and Deadwood Dick. Most shared the nobler virtues of their predecessors; but their outlaw status suggests some kind of protest against hardening class lines and the complexities and frustrations of contemporary life. These outlaws saw society as unfair and they took its injustices into their own hands. Insofar as many thousands of post-Civil War readers identified with these outlaws, they probably also identified with their rage. What has sometimes been deplored as the violent, lawless, and brutal behavior of private detectives has far deeper roots in American culture than might be supposed.

While the exact causes of this post-bellum disorientation are obviously beyond the scope of this book, it is sufficient to say that class upheavals and the economic and racial consequences of the Civil War further aggravated Ameri-cans' already fragile faith in ordinary political and social processes. At the same time the emergence of growing, bustling cities transformed life-styles and occupations. Toward the last decades of the century, a reverse migration took place from farm and countryside to the cities while, at the same time, hordes of immigrants from Asia and eastern and southern Europe began pouring into urban centers on both coasts. The popular culture reflected some of these changes in the increasing sales of detective stories that were set in cities but had heroes and villains who in some ways resembled their western counterparts.

In many of these first urban detective tales, the puzzle element was totally absent. Their plots consisted mainly of a series of adventures (often chases through city streets) in which the super-strong, super-virtuous protagonists invariably tracked down their prey. The writers therefore owed very little to the intellectual aspects of Poe's detective fiction although they did share with Poe the influence of his French contemporary, François Eugene Vidocq, a former thief, who founded the Parisian detective forces, the Sureté, and claimed to have snared many of his erstwhile criminal colleagues by donning various disguises. In his heyday, Vidocq seems to have exchanged his loyalties between the police and underworld more than once, but his *Memoirs,* published in 1828, won him wide reading audiences both in Europe and America. Poe was undoubtedly inspired to create a Parisian detective after reading Vidocq, but his M. Dupin appears much more cerebral than the shady Frenchman. On the other hand, the heroes of cheap detective fiction of the 1870s and 1880s, particularly the immensely popular Nick Carter and Old Sleuth, were, like Vidocq, masters of multiple disguise. Their tracking of criminals often led them to parts of cities seldom described in other kinds of fiction. It would be an exaggeration to describe any of these stories as realistic, but some of their more wretched settings do anticipate the slum settings of Stephen Crane and Theodore Dreiser a decade or so later.

One hero of nineteenth-century detective fiction made his debut in 1881 and survives to this day. Nick Carter, who initially worked with his father—the old sleuth, Sim Carter—still returns periodically in paperbacks, comic books, and on television. His first creator was John R. Coryell, but he had at least fifteen others, one of whom, Frederick Van Rensselaer Dey, boasted of having written a thousand titles. By 1900, fifteen hundred Nick Carter novels had been published and more than four million sold.

Nick and Sim had their rivals both in story papers and in dime novels, and some of them rejoiced in such names as Old Sleuth, Old Cap Collier, Young Badger and his father Old Badger, Deep Duke, Broadway Billy, Diamond Dick and Diamond Dick, Jr., and Old King Brady and his son, Young King. These private detectives all managed to do things the police were incapable of doing. If they often displayed amused contempt for organized authority, they nonetheless remained supporters of the social order, looking with extreme suspicion at foreigners or persons with odd-sounding names. Perhaps, at bottom, they were simply unwitting believers in the Protestant ethic, like Dashiell Hammett's Continental Op some forty years later, who did what he did because he took pride in doing his job well. In one mystery, Russel Nye quotes Nick Carter as saying he caught crooks because "that is the profession I have followed." These first detective heroes foreshadowed their hardboiled descendants in another essential way. If, on occasion, they would discover that the criminals they were pursuing were incredibly beautiful women, unyieldingly devoted to their jobs, they arrested them all the same.

Story papers began to decline in the late 1880s, due in part to the appearance of serialized fiction in Sunday newspaper supplements. Most dime novels died a decade later, largely because the costs of sending them through the mails had become prohibitive. In any case, the latter were now being read chiefly by adolescents. But formula fiction persevered in magazines produced from cheap wood pulp, the first of which, *Argosy,* was published in 1896 by Frank

Munsey. Other entrepreneurs, like Street and Smith and Frank Tousey, former publishers of dime novels and story papers, broke into the pulp field shortly thereafter. Initially pulp magazines included a variety of types of adventure fiction within their covers, but by 1920 most had become specialized and even subspecialized. For example, not only were many publications devoted to love stories, but some to "spicy" love stories; not only were other publications devoted to westerns, but some to "lariat" romances. The first pulp dedicated to detective fiction, not counting Nick Carter pulps, was *Detective Story,* founded in 1915 by Street and Smith. But it was not until 1926 that a magazine devoted itself exclusively to hardboiled detectives. This was *Black Mask* under the new editorship of Joseph Thompson Shaw. Shaw, a former World War I army captain and national champion swordman, demanded a rigorous stoic image for his action detectives and so successful was he that *Black Mask* had more than a dozen imitators through the 1930s. Few, however, matched Shaw's magazine in popularity or in the quality of its fiction.

Hardboiled private eyes made their initial appearance in *Black Mask* several years before Captain Shaw decided to confine the magazine exclusively to their heroics. Founded in 1920 by H. L. Mencken and the theater critic, George Jean Nathan, *Black Mask* originally contained short detective fiction both of the genteel puzzle variety and of the Nick Carter adventure kind. Mencken and Nathan, who regarded all pulps as so much trash (they owned others as well), sold *Black Mask* after its first six months of life, whereupon three succeeding editors, George Sutton, Phil Cody, and Harry North, began encouraging their writers to take the hardboiled road.Both Cody and North were especially important in the emerging career of Dashiell Hammett.

The first of the hardboiled detectives was Carroll John Daly's ever-violent Race Williams. Williams made his debut as an anonymous private eye in the pages of *Black Mask* in 1922, but Daly provided him with a name the following year. The writing was simplistic and sloppy even by pulp standards, yet there can be little doubt that Race's character and style set the pace for his more adroit successors. Race contributed to the detective genre the wisecrack larded with simile— "The room was as empty as a Congressman's head"— but, more important, he helped establish certain conventions. Race told his stories in the first person and had curious idiosyncrasies, like sleeping with a loaded gun in his hand. He was not without a macabre sense of humor, once explaining his random gunning down of criminals by saying, "You can't make hamburger without grinding up a little meat." He was, moreover, exceedingly suspicious of the rich and well-placed, although, as he made clear, neither did he have any use for Communists. Nor did he believe much in the efficacy or honesty of government: "There ain't nothing in government unless you're a politician, and as I said before, I ain't a crook." Like other popular heroes Race regarded himself both as an individualist and as an outsider: "You see I'm a kind of fellow in the center—not a crook, and not a policeman. Both of them look on me with suspicion. . . ."

Daly's detective can write his own rules. "Right and wrong," says Race, "are not written on the statutes for me, nor do I find my code of morals in the essays of long-winded professors." He is his own god and can bump off people with an easy conscience. "After a man has had his warning," he announces in one of his earliest manifestations, "it's good ethics to shoot him down—at least I see it that way. That is, if he needs it bad and you happen to have my code of morals." One suspects Daly's hero makes up his code in accordance with the exigencies of the plot but in certain ways he likes to think of himself as possessing the hard-nosed realism of an old-fashioned tycoon. In one story he declares that he has no intention of rendering his services free—after all, Henry Ford and John D. Rockefeller did not give away their products gratis. But if Ford and Rockefeller are culture models of sorts, it is not because they are rich, but because they are fierce individualists who refuse to be reduced by sentimentality (though like them, Race does on occasion put himself out for the weak and deserving). Finally, Daly's detective carries forward the tradition of the sexually isolated hero. Women admire Race Williams and his manly indifference to their wiles, but even when he knows they mean well, he knows also they mean trouble. When possible, he stays out of their way.

Daly and a young colleague, Erle Stanley Gardner, were the most popular *Black Mask* writers when Captain Shaw assumed his editorship in 1926, but Shaw's favorite was a third early contributor, Dashiell Hammett. One of the things Shaw liked best about Hammett was the economy of his prose, and he asked his authors to measure their writing against Hammett's. "Prune and cut," he would urge, "and don't use a single word that you can do without." Frank Gruber, a *Black Mask* writer of the 1930s, says that at its best the magazine printed the "sparest prose" of any publication in the country. Raymond Chandler, another *Black Mask* author, believed that the singular stylistic contribution of the tough detective magazine was that it returned American prose to the sounds, rhythms, and diction of ordinary speech—particularly American urban speech. (Although the best American writers have never utterly removed themselves from the spoken word, the vernacular voices of Mark Twain, Stephen Crane, Ring Lardner, and Ernest Hemingway were not distinctively urban.) Tough-guy prose helped institutionalize the wisecrack, usually in the form of a simile, and the city dweller's peculiar brand of ironic humor, usually in terms of an understated observation. Finally, *Black Mask* and pulps like it also heavily employed underworld jargon. Today much of the jargon sounds stylized and self-conscious, but at its best in Hammett and Chandler, there is a certain poetry to it that transcends its time.

Shaw was immensely proud of all his writers and managed to recruit some of the best in the field, including Frederic Nebel, Raoul Whitfield, Norbert Davis, George Harmon Coxe, Paul Cain, and Lester Dent, who purportedly wrote all the best-selling Doc Savage novels. According to Dent, Shaw had the knack of making all his contributors feel like authors rather than hacks. Moreover, he would defend them in print. Once in 1933 when *Vanity Fair,* a slick magazine, decried pulp writing as not being "real literature," Shaw took to his own editorial pages "to assert that *Vanity Fair* itself would not find too favorable a comparison between its regular fiction and article writers and those of *Black Mask*." *Black Mask* fiction, Shaw said, portrayed three-dimensional characters whose psychology was revealed through their actions. Elsewhere he wrote that underneath *Black Mask* heroes' tough exteriors lay wholesome manly idealism. But if Shaw thought of his writers as artists, he wanted *Black Mask* readers to think of them as being nearly as virile as their heroes. In one issue he listed all *Black Mask* authors who stood over six feet—but neglected to mention that one of them, Caroll John Daly, had fears about going to the dentist. Despite his success, Shaw had differences with his publishing bosses, and in 1936 he left the magazine to become a literary agent. *Black Mask* flourished a bit after his departure and still managed to print some superior authors into the 1940s, among them John D. Macdonald. But with the advent of war, real life heroes began displacing fantasy detectives and it soon became clear that the heyday of the pulps was past.

By the start of the 1950s, most of the pulp magazines had ceased publication. No longer profitable, their subject matter was taken over by comic books and television. Many of the more skilled pulp writers had long before graduated to hardcover novels or Hollywood. Some, like Mickey Spillane who combined the most lurid elements of comic books, porno magazines, and private-eye pulps (all of which he had written for), created in paper editions an unremitting caricature of the brave but cynical knights of the 1930s. At their height in the Depression years, the pulps had an estimated readership of twenty-five million readers. Their demise, like the demise of the dime novel and story paper before them, was due in part to technological changes that made other media more efficient conveyors of popular attitudes. The fate of *Black Mask* was not, however, quite like that of other pulps. During those first post-war years of precipitous decline, the magazine was "bought up" by the more refined *Ellery Queen's Mystery Magazine* whose subheading afterward read "including *Black Mask*." The publication still claims a respectable circulation and its fiction contains detectives both genteel and visceral. This magazine continues to serve as a proving ground for newer authors, including Ross Macdonald, whose first short, crime fiction was published in its pages in 1946. Some thirty years later, he would write that it "fortunately continues to sustain mystery writers between the novelists' widely separated paydays."

But if private-detective fiction still prospers, there can be little doubt that the tough-guy hero has declined. The slide began toward the end of the 1940s. Possibly the energy required to survive the Depression and the zeal required to fight World War II induced feelings of fatigue toward the detectives crusading spirit. Possibly too the growing independence of women as both breadwinners and war workers dampened readers' ardor for machismo. It may be also that the detective's cocky individualism was no longer fashionable in those first Eisenhower/McCarthy grey flannel years. For despite his old-fashioned social values, he was a reckless activist and what people seemed to want most was respite from the turmoil of the past two decades.

The respite was seldom achieved. There was a moral ambiguity in the air, relating in part to America's explosion of atomic weapons and in part to a disenchantment with wars (cold and Korean), not to mention the witch-hunts for subversives that caught up with and humiliated one of the original tough-guy writers, Dashiell Hammett. The detective operates best where the culture is surest of itself; the post-World War II years, by contrast, seemed to lack focus, and in the 1960s and 1970s racial and youth upheavals along with anti-Vietnam War sentiments did not much alter the picture. As a consequence the popular hero who took his configuration from the cultural ambiance behaved erratically.

The most celebrated tough private eye of the 1950s (and he had a few imitators in his time) was Mickey Spillane's Mike Hammer, who, as we have already remarked, reacted more violently than ever against "Reds," women, and perverts of all types whom he blamed for the unsettled American atmosphere. All the hardboiled detective's potential for sadism, anarchy, vigilantism, and god-like self-absorption is realized in the Hammer stories. Detectives like Mike Hammer are not, however, fascists as some critics have dubbed them. The disturbing aspects of their nature are latent in American popular heroes as far back as the start of the nineteenth century. What they lack is the concealed idealism, the grace under pressure, and the genuine chivalry of earlier popular figures. More disturbing than Spillane's hero are Chester Himes's brutal black cops, Coffin Ed Johnson and Grave Digger Jones. The latter, as we shall see, despair of America. For them racism is the disease that eats away at society and what few crimes they solve, they know, merely assuage an incurable illness. Indeed so contaminated is American life that in their last novel they cannot even catch the main crooks.

Still, happily, not all postwar novelists were so pessimistic. John D. Macdonald's adventurer-detective Travis McGee carries on in more traditional fashion, adjusting nicely to social and cultural ambiguities, while managing at the same time to maintain his integrity. And Ross Macdonald's Lew Archer, far less tough than the detectives of the 1930s and 1940s, seeks out a kind of middle ground lying somewhere between cultural change and the requirements of social order. Archer appears less and less happy about the human condition these days, but the balance he gropes for may well provide the direction for future private eyes.

One of the paradoxes of the popular culture is that despite its transitory nature, a few hardboiled private eyes, like Hammett's Sam Spade, and Chandler's Philip Marlowe, have survived and remain almost as popular today as they used to be. They are kept alive not only in their books, but in movies, old and new, that are constantly being replayed on television. Learned conferences at home and abroad discuss their activities, and articles and books (like this one) are written to discover their meaning. From time to time a plethora of new hardboiled detectives appear on the horizon chiefly to exploit the current interest—but on the whole they quietly fade as it becomes clear they are simply intruders on the zeitgeist.

The resurgence of interest in the private detectives is due, to a certain extent, to nostalgia. They tell us about simpler times when decisions, right and wrong, were easier to make. They tell us, too, what we would like to believe—that courage and integrity still count, and perhaps, above all, that an individual's actions make a difference: as our lives become more and more bureaucratized, we long for the clarity and decisiveness of the hardboiled hero. Yet there may be other more pervasive reasons for the enduring attractiveness of the detective hero.

To begin with, his adventures satisfy our yearnings for a good story—a story that begins at the start, follows more or less a chronological order, and comes to some kind of conclusion. However intellectually provocative we may find open-ended modern novels, we still crave the swift narration of events that fulfills our need (as it did when we were children) to find out what happens next. Moreover, a number of the hardboiled writers, despite their crude characterizations and contrived plots, knew how to tell a good story. By artfully piling one episode onto the next, they seldom gave us time to remark on their tales' absurdities.

But the essential powers of the detective story rely only slightly on its sheen of realism. Instead, the hardboiled detective novel rehearses certain near mythical patterns of action that are as old as the American experience. The tough hero, tired and cynical about all the corruption that engulfs him, nonetheless enlists himself in a cause about which he himself has doubts. In order to succeed he removes himself further and further from respectable society. He soon learns that if he is to overcome brutality, criminality, and violence he must himself become brutal, criminal, and violent—he must become one with his enemies in order to defeat them. His crimes are dedicated to the cause of justice just as the western hero's rather dubious activities were often intended to advance or secure the borders of the expanding American nation. The difference is that the westerner can get away from dirty people and his own innate savagery by riding off to the open frontier. The dick cannot. It may well be that the lawless, brutal, and violent detective captures our imagination because for a moment he (and we) are pure libido while at the same time he allows us to know that he has not given himself up entirely to savagery, but has only indulged himself long enough to do the job.

When he emerges from his underground self, he is restored to some degree of psychic health (although he and we know this is only a temporary state and that he must begin anew), and has been instrumental in bringing about some modicum of justice to an unjust society. In effect, the hardboiled hero reenacts an American mythos. Did not the first unhappy European colonists and their descendants, the frontiersmen, depart their "corrupt" societies to attack and dominate men and nature? By so doing they hoped to purify themselves and establish a higher order of civilization. Alienation, violence, and redemption characterized their movements until the continent was settled. The tough detective hero in his claustrophobic urban setting ontologically rehearses the same pattern in his narration of events.

The pattern is not peculiarly American. In myths the world over, disoriented heroes escape their societies and descend to forbidden depths only to arise and reinvigorate their ancient civilizations. But in America the conditions for the propagation of such myths have been peculiarly favorable. Here spread out before the newcomer lay an enormous continent, sparsely populated and rich in natural resources, where the moral, social, and cultural authority of Europe scarcely prevailed. And even if the new American wished to do so, he could not always consult the traditions or institutions of the European past, because they were either not available or not especially applicable. In the absence of all else, he had to fall back on himself to define his character, and he did so often by violent means. Perhaps by destroying others he was affirming his own life: "I kill, therefore I live." Lacking other definable qualities he was at least capable of surviving in a hostile or indifferent world. This is hardly an identity, but it is a start, and Americans are constantly restarting as technology, mobility, and history continue to sweep away older systems of belief, older assumptions.

The isolated, lonely hardboiled detective who is realistic about delusions of the past and the fragility of other people's assumptions sometimes represents this iconoclastic vision of an American identity. But there is also something else in his nature—the hidden idealist with his secret dream of a decent society—the tough guy with a heart of gold. Not surprisingly we find more idealistic detectives in hard times than in periods of prosperity. What this probably signifies is that the detective and his readers look at the human race with a bit more skepticism when they can afford to do so.

Any assessment of the detective's appeal must also take into account that he is a city dweller, and cities, whatever their importance as cultural and political centers, are also repositories of people and social classes whose confining, specialized activities often deny them perceptions of a larger world. In the nineteenth century, European urban novelists like Balzac and Dickens could provide readers with such an overview. They portrayed the lives and doings of individuals of varying backgrounds and attempted to relate these to one another. In effect they projected a comprehensive view of society. The creator of the tough detective takes up the mantle of his nineteenth-century urban predecessors. His hero's job is to solve crimes, and to do this he must move up and down the social ladder to make connections among persons of all social classes.

CHAPTER 2

Dashiell Hammett: Success as Failure

For aficionados, Dashiell Hammett is the father of all hardboiled detectives. Masters of the genre like Raymond Chandler, Ross MacDonald, and Chester Himes pay him homage as do any number of present-day imitators. But Hammett owed something of his style and a good deal of the mythology of the private detective to one of his "pulp" predecessors, Caroll John Daly. Moreover, during the most productive years of his career, he was bound by the dictates of his editors at *Black Mask* who imposed formulas on their authors that demanded a rigorous prose style, "realistic" characters, and plenty of action. Within these limits Hammett's reputation is deserved. He wrote better than most, his narratives are more inventive, and he possessed a sense of humor. There were, however, occasions when he verged on self-parody, and toward the end of his career he had evidently begun to feel uncomfortable with his tough heroes who were cynical, unswervingly devoted to their jobs, amoral, courageous, and seemingly impervious to emotions.

Perhaps he had come to find the genre too restricting. Some of his later pieces attempt to break with formula. Shortly after the publication of his fourth novel (*The Glass Key*, 1931), Hammett wrote Lillian Hellman that he had begun work on yet another detective novel and thought, prophetically, that it would be his last. *The Thin Man,* published in 1934, was not only Hammett's last detective novel, it was also the last major fiction he would write. Aside from a comic strip he presumably coauthored with Alex Raymond ("Secret Agent X-9"), a few radio scripts in the 1940s and 1950s based mainly on characters of his early fiction, and periodic journeys to Hollywood to "doctor" or to suggest stories for screenplays, Hammett's creative years had come to an end. Some time around the mid-1950s he wrote a thinly disguised autobiographical fragment, "Tulip" (published posthumously), in which the main character, Pop, a former detective story author, cries out: "Why can't I write?" Hammett died in January 1961.

Hammett's fallow years are their own mystery—especially when one contrasts them to his most fertile period, 1927 to 1930, during which he produced four novels and over seventy short stories. Perhaps his silence had something to do with the recharged social consciousness of the 1930s when a man's individual actions and his means of earning a living were reckoned to have public consequences. Heretofore Hammett's private eyes had happily served robber barons and the disagreeable rich who were willing to pay for their services. Their only principles were the standards of their profession. They could not be bribed or deterred from their obligations (as they saw them) by appeals to friendship, sentimentality, sex, or even romantic love. Like Hammett himself in his Pinkerton years, they took an almost primitive pleasure in the manhunt and the successful pursuit of criminals. They rarely questioned the morality of their profession or its political or social consequences. For instance, in one short story, "This King Business" (1928), Hammett's Continental Op helps to undermine a fragile Baltic republic in order to save the playboy son of his client. Such behavior on the part of Hammett's twenties heroes must have seemed the height of social irresponsibility during the early years of the Depression. In his last novel, his protagonist is a former detective, now a member of the business autocracy. As a nonprofessional he need only take a dilettantish interest in solving the crime and as a rich man he is of course pursuing his class interests in tracking down the murderer of another rich man. (Ironically, Hammett's book reviews of the late 1920s inveighed against an earlier dilettante detective, S.S. Van Dine's Philo Vance, who casually solved crimes involving persons far removed from poverty.) In *The Thin Man,* there are no characters who express the interests of the poor (mainly physical survival), except the criminals of the underworld.

Hammett's Marxism in the 1930s may also have contributed to his creative paralysis. Other writers of the Depression years evaded ideological contradictions by having their detectives criticize the rich while serving them, but Hammett did not rationalize in this fashion. The detective genre in part upholds established values by visiting fantasy punishment on its violators. If one no longer believes, what does one do? Early in their relationship, Hammett admitted to Lilliam Hellman that he had been a strikebreaker for the Pinkertons and implied he quit the detective business because an official of Anaconda Copper had asked him to kill a union organizer. Hammett refused but learned later that the organizer had been lynched anyway. One can only conjecture how Hammett reacted. Were hunter and hunted cut from the same cloth? So long as he managed to keep polarities in balance, Hammett would remain a detective. When he could not, he became a writer. The same sort of questions must have plagued him as a writer. By giving himself over to ideological commitments, he may have resolved his doubts, but in so doing he probably relinquished the kind of tensions his work required.

Some of these tensions are demonstrated in tales in which his heroes express skepticism about ever discovering truth or order. Their view of society as being inherently corrupt and unknowable is not affectation; society is ultimately a metaphor of their universe. In order to survive they betray, deceive, and kill, but the truths they ferret out very often resemble the lies they have uncovered. When Hammett reached out in these directions, he appears to be challenging formula. But whether or not he succeeded is another question.

Hammett was born a Catholic of old American stock in St. Mary's County, Maryland on May 25, 1894. His family was poor and Hammett left school at the age of fourteen to take odd jobs. His status was peculiar: he was both an insider and an outsider, not unlike the all-knowing and classless detectives he would later write about. As an insider he was a securely rooted white Southerner (and there is more than a touch of class and race arrogance in his early fiction), but he was also an outsider because he was poor and Catholic in a society devoted to the Protestant success ethic. Hammett probably dropped out of school because of his philandering father's inadequacy as a provider, and there is reason to believe Hammett felt bitter for a long time afterward. He signed some of his first published pieces "Peter Collinson"—in underworld argot, Peter Collins means "nobody,"—identifying himself to the cognoscenti as nobody's son. A psychoanalytical approach might explain Hammett's fictional supervirile heroes as being alter egos who compensated for a weak father. By the same token, the manhunt in Hammett's fiction may be regarded as the search for and destruction of the father.

At twenty-one Hammett answered an advertisement in a Baltimore newspaper and joined the Pinkerton Detective Agency. What it was about him that appealed to his prospective employers we cannot tell, but he was obviously of impeccable native ancestry (the Pinkertons were at that time fearful of foreign agitators) and, according to Lillian Hellman, remarkably self-possessed, even as a youngster. Hammett never says why he wanted to become a detective, but as a Pinkerton plainsclothesman he played roles both as an insider who worked to preserve the status quo and as an outsider who pretended to work against accepted social arrangements. As a celebrity in the 1930s, he became a radical and reversed these roles; his apparent success marked him as an insider, but in actuality he was intellectually and ideologically opposed to the established order.

Fifteen months after the United States entered the First World War, Hammett enlisted in the Motorized Ambulance Corps in Baltimore but fell ill during the influenza epidemic and later developed tuberculosis. He was discharged in 1919 and resumed work with the Pinkerton agency, first in Baltimore and then in Spokane, Washington. But there were recurrences of his tuberculosis and he was twice required to convalesce in government hospitals. During one of these hospital stays he met a nurse, Josephine Dolan, whom he married in July 1921. Still debilitated by illness, Hammett was by then living in San Francisco where he was working part-time as a Pinkerton operative. The following October, Josephine gave birth to a daughter. Financially hard pressed, Hammett resigned a few months later to try his hand at writing. One of his ambitions was to write poetry.

Hammett rarely alludes to his postwar hospital stays or to much of anything else painful in his life. Perhaps as someone who sought meaning in stoic endurance he felt embarrassed by these experiences. In the post-humously published "Tulip"—a kind of fictionalized autobiographical frag-ment—he seems unable to make any sense of his sufferings.

> I've been in a couple of wars—or at least in the army while they were going on—and in federal prisons and I had t.b. for seven years and have been married as often as I chose and have had children and grandchildren and except for one fairly nice but pointless brief story about a lunger going to Tijuana for an afternoon and evening holiday from his hospital near San Diego I've never written a word about any of these things. Why? All I can say is they're not for me. Maybe not yet, maybe not ever. I used to try now and then—and I suppose I tried hard, the way I tried a lot of things—but they never came out meaning very much to me.

During the years of Hammett's Pinkerton employment, the agency func-tioned as a sort of national police force whose operatives were licensed to make arrests (there would be no FBI until 1924). Founded as a spy agency for the North during the Civil War, Pinkerton expanded its activities nation-wide to include services to large corporations, banks, and insurance com-panies. Not surprisingly, its structure and interests came to resemble those of its big business clients; by Hammett's time the agency had long been known for its antiunion activities. But it also dealt with suspected criminals and the organized underworld. In England it was known as America's Scotland Yard, an invisible arm of government.

Lillian Hellman says that when she first met Hammett in 1930, he still bore the scars of struggles with criminals. But when Hammett reminisced in print about his experiences, his stories were, in the main, amusing. He tells of arresting a man who stole a ferris wheel, and of "shadowing" a man who got lost in the country and asked him the way back to the city. He speaks of following Fanny Brice about in hopes of discovering the whereabouts of her gangster husband, Nickie Arnstein, and how he worked on behalf of the film comedian, Fatty Arbuckle, who, he says, was falsely maligned by news-papers in a sex scandal. Hammett capitalized on his Agency experiences by presenting himself as an authority on crime. In the back pages of *Black Mask* he sometimes "wrote" letters to the editor about criminal psychology and correct methods of criminal procedure. He never wrote about being a strike-breaker.

One story Hammett tells about himself is worth repeating because, whether true or not, it throws light on his character. He was beginning to find detective work dull and had long dreamed of visiting Australia. One day he was assigned to track down a missing allotment of gold and learned subse-quently that it was being smuggled aboard an Australia-bound liner. He searched the ship with no success and therefore packed his bags and prepared for an ocean voyage. On the day of departure he made one more search and, to his dismay, found the gold cached away in a smokestack. Crushed by his success, he returned the gold to its owners and tendered his resignation to the Pinkertons.

The failure of success—the way success imperils one's dreams—is a theme that runs through Hammett's life and work. His detective stories anticipate the ironies of triumph that we see in the paralysis of his career when, at the height of his success, he found himself unable to write. In *The Maltese Falcon* (1930) the hero learns that the woman he loves is a cold-blooded murderess. In *The Glass Key* (1931), a young woman who is about to run off to New York with the protagonist, Ned Beaumont, tells him of a dream in which she and Beaumont desperately try to enter a house. They succeed, but the glass key with which they turn the lock breaks, and hideous snakes slither out the door. It is not always fortunate that dreams come true.

Five years after he left the Pinkertons, Hammett left home. He feared his occasional tubercular relapses would infect his younger daughter born in May 1926. But Hammett, like the father he despised, was also something of a womanizer, and domestic tensions probably contributed to his departure. There were reconciliations from time to time, but by 1929 his separation from wife and children was permanent.

Neither Hammett's illnesses nor his marital difficulties seem to have affected his literary output. His first short stories appeared in *Smart Set* in 1922 and he produced thereafter a steady flow of fiction, mainly for *Black Mask*. In 1926 he wrote advertising copy for a San Francisco jeweler and the following year published articles about the "art" of advertising. A few of his poems and a couple of book reviews were also published in 1927. But Hammett's reputation as a writer rested on his crime fiction.

The first of his thirty-six Continental Op stories was printed in October 1923. All but two would be published in *Black Mask;* the last, "Death and Company," appeared in November 1930. Eight of the stories he revised for his novels *Red Harvest* and *The Dain Curse.* In addition, he wrote roughly forty non-Op stories between 1923 and 1934,most of which were printed in *Black Mask.* Nine of these he revised for *The Maltese Falcon* and *The Glass Key.* A slightly abridged version of *The Thin Man* was printed in the slick *Redbook* in 1933. It was the only Hammett novel that did not make its debut in the more proletarian pulps.

Not all of Hammett's early narratives dealt with crime and detection. One or two were westerns and some simply "adventure," but even these hint at the thwarted romanticism that characterizes his later writings. In one story, "The Crusader" (1923), a Ku Klux Klansman stands in front of a mirror admiring himself in his white robes. He imagines himself as a Crusader or Sir Galahad. The gap between his pathetic fantasies and the banality of his life becomes apparent when a little boy enters the room and, thinking him dressed for a child's game, cries out, "Peekaboo!"

In another story, "The Road Home" (1922), a New York detective, Hagedorn, has finally after two years apprehended the fugitive jewel thief, Barnes, in the jungles of Burma. Although Barnes cannot bribe the detective, he manages to escape anyway by jumping off a small boat that is taking them downriver. Hagedorn realizes that it may well take him another five years before he catches up with Barnes. He could of course allow the dark skinned native "muggars" who wait along the shore to kill the fugitive but then "the sudden logical instinct to side with the member of his own species against enemies from another wiped out all other considerations, and sent his rifle to his shoulder to throw a shower of bullets into the *muggars*." The story, brief as it is, foreshadows themes of some of Hammett's more mature efforts: the integrity of the detective (he cannot be bribed), the detective's racism (nonwhites generally appear as inferiors or antagonists in Hammett's works), a real jungle in anticipation of the city as jungle, and, finally, the bittersweet ending where the detective allows his success to fail.

Hammett's romanticism also extends to his portrayal of women. In the Op stories they rarely deter his hero, a pudgy, middle-aged detective, from performing his job efficiently. Usually they are either innocents in distress like the hapless Gabrielle in *The Dain Curse* who wrongly believes she is doomed, or beautiful criminals and seductresses like Princess Zhukowski in "The Gutting of Couffignal" (1925) who tries to loot the homes of millionaires. In the former story the hero chivalrously (and sexlessly) saves her; in the latter, the Op shoots. Shooting or arresting beautiful women may strike the reader as the obverse side of sentimentality, but here possibly lies the hidden Hammett, the soured romantic parading as a tough guy.

By 1924 Hammett's stories were featured in *Black Mask* with considerable fanfare. The often lurid covers would announce a new story by Hammett accompanied by an "action" illustration vaguely suggesting its contents. In late 1929, after the publication of his first two novels, Hammett felt secure enough financially to leave San Francisco. He came to New York to live but returned almost immediately to California on learning that Paramount Studios had bought the rights to *Red Harvest.* This would be the first of many trips to Hollywood ostensibly to help transform his writings into movies or to work on screenplays of other writers. A rather mangled version of *Red Harvest* was produced after his first visit, but while in Hollywood Hammett met Lillian Hellman (then married to the writer Arthur Kober), who would remain his closest friend until his death in 1961. Hammett returned to New York later that year to continue work on what turned out to be *The Thin Man* and Miss Hellman joined him shortly thereafter.

The future looked rosy. Hammett's lucrative relationship with Hollywood would continue for the next twenty years. In addition to his work on screenplays, each of his other novels (with the exception of *The Dain Curse*) and three of his short stories would be made into films. The movie of *The Thin Man* (1934) featuring William Powell and Myrna Loy was so successful that five sequels were made, the last one being produced in 1947. The *Maltese Falcon* was made twice in the 1930s and once again in John Huston's famous 1941 version with Humphrey Bogart and Mary Astor, and *The Glass Key* was made twice, once in 1935 and again in 1942. A 1940s radio serial, "The Fat Man" to which Hammett had lent his name, was also made into a movie. Despite these successes, Hollywood seems to have affected his performance as a writer. After his first visit, Hammett wrote little more tough-guy fiction.

Hammett's last thirty years are chronicled impressionistically in Lillian Hellman's reminiscences. At the start, a good portion of their time was spent away from New York, drinking, hunting, and fishing. Hammett was reserved and self-contained and not given much to elaborating on his views, political or otherwise. If he was disturbed that he was unable to write, he did not show it. He had a few literary friends—Nathaniel West, William Faulkner, S. J. Perelman, and Ben Hecht—but they were not so celebrated at the time, and one gathers they did not talk much about their work. Hammett did not like literary palaver although he had catholic interests and read widely. Hellman writes that he was capable of exercising self-discipline and tells about extended periods in which he locked himself in a hotel room in order to finish *The Thin Man*. But the novel was no longer than his others and, judging from other evidence, must have taken him at least three years to write. What Hammett may have done is transfer his creative energies to Hellman—or more properly, her playwriting. He encouraged her to write, read and reread her manuscripts, and honestly gave his opinions. Whatever else their years together meant, he comes across most distinctly as a mentor and critic.

In 1937 or 1938 Hammett joined the Communist party. This was hardly a propitious moment since many intellectuals were at that time dropping their Party affiliations in reaction to the Moscow Purge Trials. But Hammett now participated in or lent his name to a number of publicized left-wing causes. Hellman says that although he was skeptical about Party rhetoric and policies, he felt there was no better alternative. In 1942, after the United States' entry into World War II, Hammett reenlisted in the army at the age of forty-eight. He served as a sergeant in one of the more remote Aleutian Islands editing an army newspaper. Perhaps because the experience was so different from the kind of life he had been living in New York and Hollywood, he truly enjoyed it. He was evidently popular with the troops who called him "Pop" and looked to him for advice and reassurance. When he was discharged in 1945, he began drinking even more heavily than before—so much so that after a couple of years, Lillian Hellman says that she could no longer live with him. The following year his doctors warned him that he was endangering his life. Although the prognosis for a middle-aged alcoholic was not favorable, Hammett stopped drinking and for all intents and purposes remained a teetotaler to the end of his life. In 1951 he was called before a United States District Court where he was asked to identify some of the sponsors of the left-wing Civil Rights Congress. Hammett probably did not even know their names but he refused to answer on principle and was thereupon remanded to federal prison. When he was released six months later, Lillian Hellman saw a genuinely sick man.

Although he was uncomplaining and joked about it afterwards, Hammett's imprisonment must have gone badly for him. His fictional private eyes had been upholders of America in their fashion. In all probability, they emerged in part as a fantasy reaction to fears that constitutional processes were inadequate to cope with criminals. Hammett may have believed that his Communism was the logical extension of democratic principles. His refusal to answer the Court's questions proved as much from his point of view. Moreover, had he not twice enlisted in the American army in time of war—and could he not trace his ancestors back to the birth of the republic? Ironically, this most American of writers was now being branded a pariah by his countrymen.

Things went badly after that. He had developed emphysema in prison and found he could no longer adequately take care of himself. Meanwhile the government had placed a lien on his royalties for nonpayment of back taxes amounting to more than $111,000. He was very nearly impoverished. After a few years he went back to live with Lillian Hellman. He tried to write about himself but the fragmentary "Tulip" was evasive. He became more and more of a recluse. Once Lillian Hellman came upon him in tears (the only time), but he told her he did not want to talk to her, that his only chance was to work things out by himself. This was what he truly believed, whatever his professed social and political views: ultimately one is alone, like all the stoic, battered heroes of his fiction. In the throes of death—he would die of lung cancer in January 1961—he refused medication. He asked to be buried in Arlington National Cemetry.

Hammett's tough-guy fiction represents the marriage of two kinds of popular writing that had been developing in America since the nineteenth century: the novel of detection derived from Poe, and the western adventure derived from James Fenimore Cooper. The Poe-like puzzle element requiring some kind of intellectual effort on the part of the detective is not altogether absent in Hammett's stories, but it gives way more often than not to suspenseful episodic adventures replete with violence and danger to the hero. One of Hammett's contributions to the genre is that he rendered popular adventure more plausible by making the detection seem realistic—mental acuteness is preceded by solid plodding investigation. In "The Girl With The Silver Eyes" (1924), for example, the Op tracks down a missing girl by checking out bank statements, taxi trip records, railroad ticket purchases, and even weather reports. Without question Hammett brought his professional experience to bear on this kind of fiction, but he was also one of the rare pulp writers capable of conveying a feeling for character. It was not simply that he gave murder back to real murderers (to paraphrase Raymond Chandler), but he gave them style, speech, and dress. Their brutality and avarice were a part of their natures and not something grafted onto dull people to surprise the reader. Hammett had a good ear for underworld jargon.

I went gunning for Holy Joe. I knew him but didn't know where he jungled up, and didn't find out till yesterday. You was there when I came. You know about that. I had picked up a boiler and parked it over on Turk Street, for the getaway. When I got back to it, there was a copper standing close to it. I figured he might have spotted it as a hot one and was waiting to see who came for it, so I let it alone, and caught a streetcar instead, and cut for the yards. Down there I ran into a whole flock of hammer and saws and had to go overboard in China Basin. . . ." ["Flypaper," 1929]

But Hammett was also proficient in rendering other people besides hoodlums. Consider, for example, the fat man, Gutman, an obviously educated mercantile type desperately anxious to possess a carved bird known as the Maltese Falcon. Hammett's description reads like Dickens.

The fat man was flabbily fat with bulbous pink cheeks and lips and chins and neck, with a great soft egg of a belly that was all his torso, and pendant cones for arms and legs. As he advanced to meet Spade all his bulbs rose and shook and fell separately with each step, in the manner of clustered soap bubbles not yet released from the pipe through which they had been blown. His eyes, made small by fat puffs around them, were dark and sleek. Dark ringlets thinly covered his broad scalp. He wore a black cutaway coat, black vest, black satin Ascot tie holding a pinkish pearl, striped grey worsted trousers, and patent-leather shoes. His voice was a throaty purr. "Ah, Mr. Spade," he said with enthusiasm and held out a hand like a fat pink star.

When the detective, Sam Spade, asks him whether he wants to talk about the bird, Gutman responds with a kind of Dickensian exuberance.

"Will we?" he asked and, "We will," he replied. His pink face was shiny with delight. "You're the man for me, sir, a man cut along my own lines. No beating about the bush, but right to the point. 'Will we talk about the black bird?' We will. I like that, sir. I like that way of doing business. Let us talk about the black bird by all means. . . ."

Unfortunately Hammett was also capable of employing the most simpleminded racial stereotypes. The bad Indians of the popular westerns often become the bad Africans, Negroes, homosexuals, and Orientals in Hammett's mythology.

The Chinese are a thorough people; if any one of them carries a gun at all, he usually carries two or three or more. . . . Once more Tai ran true to racial form. When a Chinese shoots he keeps on until his gun is empty. ["The House on Turk Street," 1924]

In lieu of the monosyllabic grunts or stilted rhetoric of pulp Indians, Hammett substitutes the clever, exaggerated politeness of vaudeville Chinese:

If the Terror of Evildoers will honor one of my deplorable chairs by resting his divine body on it, I can assure him the chair shall be burned afterward, so no lesser being may use it. Or will the Prince of Thief-catchers permit me to send a servant to his palace for a chair worthy of him? ["Dead Yellow Women," 1925.]

In *Red Harvest,* the Op has a disturbing dream of a "brown man" who becomes a symbol of elusive evil.

> I was in a strange city hunting for a man I hated. I had an open knife in my pocket and meant to kill him. . . .

The streets are full and church bells are ringing. Suddenly the Op sees him.

> He was a small brown man who wore an immense sombrero. He was standing on the steps of a tall building on the far side of a wide plaza, laughing at me.

The Op chases him up miles of stairs to a roof.

> My hand knocked his sombrero off, and closed on his head. It was a smooth hard round head no larger than a large egg. My fingers went all the way around it. Squeezing his head in one hand, I tried to bring the knife out of my pocket with the other.

As in the dime novels and formula westerns, perpetrators of violence (and hence objects of violence) are often dark-skinned peoples who attempt to stem the westward advance of white American civilization.

Hammett's detective, like the western hero, is an outsider who feels ambivalent about the society he is defending. For him women represent society both in its ideal aspects (domesticity and civilization) and its negative side (corruption and restraint); despite his facade of detachment and devotion to duty, he may be forced to display his anger towards women overtly:

> "Stop, you idiot!" I bawled at her.
> Her face laughed over her shoulder at me. She walked without haste to the door, her short skirt of grey flannel shaping itself to the calf of each gray wool stockinged leg. . . .
> "Adieu!" she said softly.
> And I put a bullet in the calf of her left leg.
> She sat down—plump! Utter surprise stretched her white face. It was too soon for pain.
> I had never shot a woman before. I felt queer about it.
>   ["The Gutting of Couffignal," 1925]

Another connection between the western hero and the detective is the almost magical role each plays in purging the community of its evil members. At least two of Hammett's short stories ("Corkscrew," 1925, and "The Farewell Murder," 1930) and one of his novels, *Red Harvest,* take place in remote western territory into which the Op comes as a stranger; he solves crimes, and then withdraws as would any lone ranger. Neither the Hammett detective nor the westerner regards human behavior as complicated. Most bad men and criminals act out of simple motives—avarice, fear, lust, or power. Elaborate webs of psychoanalytical theory are simply shrouds for the obvious. In *The Dain Curse,* the villain, an author who is in some respects the Op's (and Hammett's) alter ego, writes an article for the *Psychopatho-logical Review* "condemning the hypothesis of an unconscious or subconscious mind as a snare and a delusion, a pitfall for the unwary and a set of false whiskers for the charlatan." Later the Op explains a murderer's violence as simply "dislike for being thwarted, spitefulness when trapped."

But if they are behaviorists, Hammett's characters are also idealists in their fashion. In the absence of anything else to believe in, the detectives believe in their jobs to which they gladly sacrifice themselves and even their lovers.

> I pass up about twenty-five or thirty thousand of honest gain because I like being a detective, like the work. And liking work makes you want to do it as well as you can. Otherwise there'd be no sense to it. That's the fix I'm in. I don't know anything else, don't enjoy anything else. . . . You think I'm a man and you're a woman. That's wrong. I'm a manhunter and you're something that has been running in front of me. There's nothing human about it. ["The Gutting of Couffignal"]

Even Hammett's nondetective hero, Ned Beaumont of *The Glass Key,* an aide to a city machine boss, has created for himself a sense of identity that no amount of brutal beatings can make him relinquish. Hammett's villains are also possessed. The author-villain Fitzstephan of *The Dain Curse* weaves elaborate criminal plots not for material gain, but for the transcendent pleasures he derives from seeing them fulfilled. The evil seekers of *The Maltese Falcon* appear transported beyond mere greed; for them the Falcon is an icon they pursue as zealously as any medieval knight pursued the grail. What ultimately motivates them defies rational explanation. Many of Hammett's possessed and obsessed characters ring truer than his earth-bound materialists or ethnic stereotypes.

Hammett's humor is often larger than life and so rises above the level of the commonplace. Consider, for example, the tall-tale quality of the following collection of corpses the Op has stumbled upon.

> There was the Dis-and-Dat Kid, who had crushed out of Leavenworth only two months before; Sheeny Holmes; Snohomish Shitey, supposed to have died a hero in France in 1919; L. A. Slim, from Denver, sockless and underwear-less as usual, with a thousand-dollar bill sewed in each shoulder of his coat; Spider Girrucci wearing a steel-mesh vest under his shirt and a scar from crown to chin where his brother had carved him years ago; Old Pete Best, once a congressman; Nigger Vojan, who once won $175,000 in a Chicago crap game—*Abracadabra* tattooed on him in three places; Alphabet Shorty McCoy; Tom Brooks, Alphabet Shorty's brother-in-law, who invented the Richmond razzle-dazzle and bought three hotels with the profits; Red Cudahy, who stuck up a Union Pacific train in 1924; Denny Burke; Bull McGonickle, still pale from fifteen years in Joliet; Toby the Lugs, Bull's running-mate, who used to brag about picking President Wilson's pocket in a Washington vaudeville theater; and Paddy the Mex. ["The Big Knockover," 1927]

Hammett was also capable of rendering both the urban wisecrack ("She's a tough little job who probably was fired for dropping her chewing gum in the soup the last place she worked") and the banter of sophisticates:

> "Whatever you're giving me [for Christmas]," she said, "I hope I don't like it."
> "You'll have to keep them anyway because the man at the Aquarium said he positively cannot take them back. He said they'd already bitten the tails off the—" [*The Thin Man*]

But Hammett is at his best when he draws together a sense of western irreverence with laconic city cynicism.

> I first heard Personville called Poisonville by a red-haired mucker named Hickey Dewey in the Big Ship in Butte. He also called his shirt a shoit. I didn't think anything of what he had done to the city's name. Later I heard men who could manage their r's give it the same pronunciation. I still didn't see anything in it but the meaningless sort of humor that used to make richardsnary the thieves' word for dictionary. A few years later I went to Personville and learned better. [*Red Harvest*]

Red Harvest is usually considered Hammett's first full length work. Set in a remote Montana mining town, the novel seems to partake of the raw western energy of its background. It is structured episodically (betraying its magazine origins once or twice), but it is always swift moving and violent, piling up at least thirty-five corpses. In some ways it modifies Daly's *Black Mask* formula. The Op, an employee of the Continental Detective Agency, is invited to Personville by a crusading newspaper editor who is murdered the night the Op arrives. The Op first clears up the killing (it was a crime of passion) and then stays on to purge the town of its all-pervading corruption. Iago-like, he manipulates each of the criminal factions that run the city—the police, the gamblers, and bootleggers—so that each sees the other as enemy. Most of them kill one another off in wild scenes of street mayhem. *Red Harvest* is a powerful adventure, but beyond the suspense lies Hammett's nightmare vision of a society completely and irreversably immersed in evil. As the tale draws to a close the Op tells the ruthless old capitalist who owns Personville that he will have his "city back nice and clean and ready to go to the dogs again."

Hammett's second novel, *The Dain Curse* is very different from its predecessor. There are no gangs and its criticism is directed mainly against fashionable religious cults and publicity-hungry politicians. The book is divided into three loosely related novellas, each of which provides the Op with several murders to solve and a suffering heroine, Gabrielle Legge, to comfort. She fears she is cursed but needless to say she is not, for the Op discovers the external source of her trouble in the final pages. The least successful of the Hammett works, it contains many hackneyed elements: missing diamonds, missing servants, superstitious mulattoes, family curses, long-lost relatives suddenly reappearing, "ghosts," and even an escape from a desert island. The novel undoubtedly represents an attempt to break away from the hardboiled formula, but in so doing it stumbles onto a nest of romantic cliches.

What is most interesting about *The Dain Curse* is the Op's vision of an illusory universe. Each of the puzzles he confronts suggests a variety of solutions. The Op's antagonists offer up any number of false answers but he is not deceived. Yet the answers the Op asks us to believe are really no more plausible than the ones he has rejected. Further, each of his solutions leads to a deeper, more mysterious puzzle. The truth can scarcely ever be known— unless one assumes faith in the always skeptical Op.

The prime liars in Hammett's writings are women and the prime liar of all Hammett's women is Brigid O'Shaugnessy of *The Maltese Falcon.* She does not succeed in deceiving Sam Spade, Hammett's new detective hero, because liars depend on believers and Sam believes only in his job. He signals his skepticism early in the novel when he tells Brigid a story about a respectable businessman, Flitcraft, who had figured in one of his investigations. Flitcraft had been a believer in an orderly universe until one day a loose beam from an office building very nearly felled him on the sidewalk below. Flitcraft told Spade he felt as if "somebody had taken the lid off life and let him look at the works." He suddenly realized that all his assumptions about an ordered rational existence were delusions. Flitcraft therefore determined that he too would live in an arbitrary and random fashion, and he abandoned his wife and children in the process. But after a while, he unconsciously slipped back into another smug bourgeois life pattern. Spade, however, does not allow himself such an indulgence. He knows life is unpredictable and he is fearless because he has adjusted himself to the fact that death is omnipresent, which gives him great power over others who take being alive too seriously.

Despite its pulp origins, *The Maltese Falcon* reads like a traditional, well-made novel. There are fewer characters than in Hammett's other works and the plot is more centered, dealing mainly with the pursuit of the murderer of Sam's partner and the activities of an international gang of jewel thieves intent on acquiring a jeweled bird. Their account of its dismal history, reaching back centuries, reads like a metaphor of Western avarice. Fittingly, when the bird is recovered they find it is false—a fitting symbol of what its pursuers have become—predatory and perfidious. Perhaps, too, the falcon has a sadder meaning. Ross Macdonald, who named his hero, Lew Archer, after Sam Spade's murdered partner, suggests that the bird may stand "for the Holy Ghost itself, or for its absence."

The novel attempts to break with the detective formula in other ways as well. Killings take place offstage, deemphasizing the violence, and the tale is told in the third person, unlike the stories the Op tells about himself. Sam Spade is given more of an individual existence than the Op. We see Sam's rooms, the clothes he wears, and his over-all appearance—tall, lean, blonde, and "saturnine," not unlike pictures of the young Hammett. Sam even takes Brigid to bed—a violation of the Op's principles, but unlike the Op,

Spade is something of a lady's man—and on one occasion he actually gets angry when a policeman knocks him about a bit. But beneath these superficial differences, Sam possesses the same ruthless character as the Op. He is as unmoved by the threats of killers as he is by the importunities of women. Thus he can surrender Brigid to the police because, even though he loves her, his code comes first.

In Hammett's next novel, *The Glass Key,* the man-woman stuff is under better control although one is left wondering why at the end of the book the hero and a young woman decide to pack off together when they hardly know one another. Indeed why the hero does any number of things is nearly as much a puzzle as the actions of the criminal characters. The narrative revolves around Ned Beaumont, an aide and friend to a city machine boss, Paul Madvig. Madvig is threatened by a rival political organization financed by the city's leading bootlegger. He is also threatened by the scandal of an unsolved murder of a senator's son, which is doubly embarrassing because Madvig wants to marry the senator's daughter. In the course of the tale Ned Beaumont successfully confronts and defeats the opposition—like the Op, he lies, betrays, and goads his enemies to suicide and shootouts— and eventually uncovers the murderer, the senator himself. But in so doing he is brutally beaten and finds he cannot even trust his friend. In the end he severs his ties with Madvig and goes off with his girl.

One of the difficulties with the novel is that its third-person narration obscures what Ned thinks or feels. We are not sure why Ned takes his bloody beatings: Is it because of his loyalties to Madvig or because his pride is injured? He has evidently fashioned a sense of himself that others cannot touch, but we are not sure what that is. Nor do we know what he did in the past or where he will go in the future. At one juncture he appears ready to sell out Madvig—would he have?—and at another to fight with Madvig over what seems a trivial difference. Did Beaumont stage the fight to delude the enemy? The quesitons are never adequately answered because Hammett seldom allows us to penetrate Beaumont's shell. More the pity, since Hammett apparently intended to give a fuller portrayal of Beaumont than any of his previous heroes. He drinks considerably, he is extremely anxious about his luck (so much so that he pursues a welshing bookie to New York), and he appears to have an intense relationship with Madvig. Hammett gives him vulnerabilities that suggest inner turmoil, but we only see these from the outside.

The novel is rich in the atmosphere of the "clubhouse" where dubious businessmen, machine bosses, elected officials, and their seedier hangers-on make sordid deals, dividing and redividing power and loot. Here Hammett reveals a sure feel for the "class" psychology of some of his characters. For example, it is clear from the start that Madvig—of uncertain ethnic origin—is fascinated by the aristocratic aura that seems to him to envelop the senator and his daughter. The senator is as crooked as everyone else, but the Henrys' "respectability" and social standing blind the otherwise worldly, ambitious city boss. One wonders whether Hammett was thinking of Fitzgerald's Gatsby when he drew Madvig; like Gatsby, Madvig is caught up in a dying American dream. His success assures his failure—which might read as an epitaph for Hammett.

Some time before the book publication of *The Glass Key,* Hammett had begun work on another hardboiled novel. He evidently changed his mind about it on several occasions because *The Thin Man* (1933) is a far cry from the somber work he had begun a couple of years before. That Hammett had by now achieved some kind of respectability may be adduced from the fact that it was first serialized in the mass circulation *Redbook.* A concession Hammett evidently made to his new readership was to agree to the removal of the word "erection" which his hero may or may not have had while wrestling with one of the women in the novel. In the interests of art, presumably, the word was returned to the hard cover text.

The novel tells about the former detective, Nick Charles, and his wife Nora, of San Francisco, who are in New York for what appears to be an alcoholic vacation. Nick, who is now basking in his wife's wealth, finds himself enmeshed in an investigation of a missing inventor who had once been a client. Drawing on some of his old detective talents as well as his knowledge of the inventor's family and friends, he proceeds to solve the mystery. But Nick is no longer the hardboiled detective (if ever he had been). Instead he is slick and witty and good at repartee—which suggests Hammett's work at Hollywood studios could not have been a total loss. Nick's wife, Nora, said to have been modelled on Lillian Hellman, is equally witty and intelligent. Underlying the bright surface of *The Thin Man* prose is a comedy of manners about New York's upper-middle drinking classes near the end of Prohibition. Most of them were unhappy. The novel was a huge success and should have provided Hammett the wherewithal to write the "serious" book he had always promised himself he would do.

Which returns us once more to Hammett's creative hiatus after *The Thin Man.* Like the alcoholic Nick, he appears to have given up on the things he did best. The fierce vigor was gone and the fame and attention would now be Lillian Hellman's. Did he will this or did his successes render him impotent? Had he taken prizes his heroes would have scorned? There are mysteries about Hammett, one feels, that neither the Op nor Sam Spade would have been able to solve.

CHAPTER 3

Raymond Chandler: The Smell of Fear

Raymond Chandler was Hammett's principal successor—his melancholy, tough-talking hero, Philip Marlowe, is one of the best-known and widely imitated popular heroes of the 1940s. Marlowe is a six-foot-tall, thirty-eight-year-old bachelor who works for himself because he is too much of an individualist to take orders from others. He is not very successful financially—his office is somewhat shabby and his living quarters spare—not because he cannot find clients but because he can be neither bought off nor scared off by the rich, the police, or by gangsters. He respects courage and physical endurance and tells us he has no use for homosexuals. His integrity and his laconic wit are his armor, but in a corrupt world he can be very lonely. The vulnerabilities with which his creator endowed him were Chandler's own, and are among the things that make him attractive.

Chandler's is a curious case. Although we like to think of him as writing quintessentially American stuff, his outlook was far more English than might ordinarily be supposed. His detectives, for all their presumed toughness, entertain Victorian notions of honor and self-sacrifice that Hammett's Op would have found amusing. Chandler was the more sophisticated stylist, although he did not possess Hammett's storytelling logic. For Chandler, scene and atmosphere were far more important than plausibility; Hammett, on the other hand, regarded plot as the most essential element of his fiction and seldom sacrificed narrative for melodramatic moments. The differences in the educational backgrounds of the two men are also striking. If Hammett was largely self-taught—accruing thereby certain primitive literary strengths—Chandler attended schools in England and France from whose formalities he may have suffered as much as he benefited. Hammett's education or lack of it contributed to more hardbitten, pragmatic attitudes. In his pre-Marxist writing years, as we have observed, he toyed with the idea of a senseless universe governed by jungle ethics, but Chandler, whose English schooling imbued him with a sterner sense of purpose, ultimately rejected such a view as nihilistic. Consequently Chandler was the more compassionate of the two, betraying greater concern for the bittersweet in human relationships. As children, both lacked strong male figures with whom they could identify, and in their adult years they enjoyed reputations as womanizers, whether merited or not. Both drank so heavily they required medical attention. Oddly, their paths crossed only once—at a reunion dinner for *Black Mask* writers in 1936. Although Chandler was an admirer of Hammett, neither spoke much to the other. One suspects they both were too shy.

Chandler was born in Chicago in 1888, two years after the wedding of his parents. His father, Maurice, a railroad engineer, was born of Quaker and Irish-American stock, but his Anglo-Irish mother, née Florence Dart Thornton, had only recently come to America from Waterford, Ireland. The Chandlers lived for several years in a small town in Nebraska, but the marriage did not take, and in 1896 Mrs. Chandler returned to Europe with her young son in tow. For the next fifteen years Raymond and his mother lived with his aunt, Ethel, and his maternal grandmother, Annie, in genteel but far from fashionable sections of London—a source of never-ending irritation to his grandmother who had known better days as an upper-class Protestant living in Ireland. Chandler remembered Annie more than fifty years later as a "stupid and arrogant" snob who worshipped wealth. Yet some of that snobbery may have rubbed off on her grandson who in 1955 described some of the first Americans he met on his return to the States as "canaille." Philip Marlowe's loathing of the phoney rich as well as the coarse and vulgar lower classes may also owe something to Chandler's grandmother.

Young Raymond passed his summer holidays in Waterford where one of grandmother Annie's sons still flourished, and here Chandler gained firsthand experience in the delicate arrangements governing Irish Catholic/Protestant relationships. (One apparently did not ask one's Catholic playmates to tea.) As an outsider—neither wholly American, English, or Irish—Raymond observed these rites with some objectivity. He was also made acutely aware of the nuances of social distinctions, an awareness he would later bring to his Los Angeles fiction. During these years his grandmother rarely allowed her daughter to forget the disgrace of her failed American marriage, arousing in Raymond the counter desire to protect and defend his mother. Florence herself no doubt reinforced her son's chivalric impulses by telling him about his American father's brutality toward her. Afterwards Chandler would speak of his mother as a "saint" and his father as an alcoholic "swine," but he may have internalized an image of his father in the philandering alcoholism of his own married years.

Perhaps Chandler's distressed heroines and violent villains are fantasy projections of his mother and father. But one must wonder whether the numerous predatory women who inhabit his fiction also reveal other attitudes towards his mother. Natasha Spender, one of Chandler's English friends of the mid-1950s, suggests that Chandler's mother made intense emotional demands on him in return for her approval. As we shall see, Chandler himself practiced a kind of emotional blackmail when, towards the end of his life, he would call his friends and tell them he would commit suicide if they did not come and minister to him at once. Interestingly, several of Chandler's short stories deal with blackmail as do all but one of his novels, but in Chandler's fiction his blackmailers are despicable—which may have been Chandler's way of expressing what he disliked about himself.

As a young man, Chandler's Galahad image of himself was probably strengthened by a class-oriented Victorian education. From 1900 to 1906 he attended Dulwich College, a preparatory school where he studied classics but also read as part of the curriculum Tennyson's Arthurian poetry and Matthew Arnold. Young scholars at Dulwich were expected to be manly, disciplined, self-sacrificing, and honorable—the same qualities of character Philip Marlowe displays some thirty years later. It was at Dulwich too that Chandler was pressed to write short sentences devoid of cumbersome adjectives under the aegis of one of the masters. Upon completing his course of studies, Chandler studied business education briefly in France and Germany (the Thorntons having determined they could not afford to send the bookish Raymond to university). A short stint in the Civil Service (the Admiralty) and a few faint forays into journalism, book reviewing, and poetry writing rounded out Chandler's remaining English years. At the age of twenty-four he headed back to the States.

It is not clear why Chandler chose to return. He was obviously no resounding success as a writer or civil servant and America may have represented another chance. Perhaps he entertained some romantic notion of rediscovering his father. Or perhaps, as one of his 1932 poems suggests, he wanted to flee a painful love affair. On his arrival in America he took odd jobs, first in St. Louis and later in Nebraska where he visited his mother's relatives. But life in the Midwest was not to his liking, and he moved on to Los Angeles where he rejoined the Lloyd family, shipboard friends whom he had met coming to America. After further desultory employment in Los Angeles, he attended three weeks of business college and with the help of the Lloyds found work as a bookkeeper in a creamery. The elder Lloyd, a lawyer and Yale Ph.D., often entertained small circles of intellectual friends at his home, and here Chandler met his future wife, Mrs. Julian Pascal (Cissy), eighteen years his senior and married at the time to a concert pianist. In 1916 Chandler's mother came to live with him. The following year he enlisted in the Canadian army. As a noncommissioned officer he led a brigade in battle and witnessed some of the carnage in France—he was the only man in his platoon to survive a German artillery barrage. Later he tried to join the Royal Air Force but the war ended and he returned to Canada where he was mustered out. According to his biographer, Frank MacShane, Chandler seldom alluded to his battle experiences afterwards. He said it was a nightmare he'd rather forget, and aside from a short unpublished sketch he wrote about a soldier under fire, there is no evidence he ever attempted war fiction. He may have transferred the fear and the horror he had known in battle to the more manageable context of the detective story, or possibly the courage and cool detachment of a platoon commander in combat are qualities not very different from those that a hardboiled detective must display under duress. In a 1957 letter recalling the war, Chandler wrote, "As a platoon commander many years ago I never seemed to be afraid, and yet I have been afraid of the most insignificant risks. If you had to go over the top somehow all you seemed to think of was trying to keep the men spaced, in order to reduce casualties."

When Chandler returned to Los Angeles in 1919 he resumed his friendship with Cissy Pascal. They had corresponded while he was away but their letters were probably platonic. When they realized they were in love, they consulted their friends and Cissy's husband (whom she claimed she still loved but not as much as she loved Raymond) and decided it would be best if Cissy obtained a divorce. This would be her second divorce—she had been married once before to a Boston businessman. In 1920 the divorce decree was granted but Chandler's mother's objections prevented their marriage. In March 1924 Chandler's mother died and two weeks later he married Cissy. Despite her age Cissy at fifty-three was still a remarkably youthful and attractive looking woman. Nonetheless the difference in years was significant and rocky times lay ahead.

Four years before his marriage, Chandler, again with the aid of the Lloyds, had obtained a minor administrative post in one of the new California oil companies. Very quickly he worked his way up to what might be termed a vice-presidency so that by the time he wed Cissy he was earning a sizable salary. He was, it appears, a rather effective executive and a stickler for principle. He went out with Cissy when circumstances demanded, but after a few years she no longer felt comfortable being seen with a man who looked so much younger, and Chandler took to making social rounds on his own. For a period the marriage appeared to founder. Chandler began drinking excessively and having affairs with some of the young women who worked in his office. He was on occasion an extremely ebullient and self-pitying drunk who once threatened to kill himself when an infuriated associate wanted to throw him out of his house for annoying his wife.

Chandler's business capabilities were inevitably affected by the changes that had come over him. Was he disenchanted with his aging wife? Given his romantic spirit, did he find his business success tedious and unfulfilling? Today it would be said that he faced a "mid-life crisis." There were days he simply did not appear at his office. He was warned. He persisted. In 1932 he was fired. Afterwards he would claim he was let go because of office politics, and at the height of his popularity as a writer he told interviewers he was fired because of the depression. His colleagues knew otherwise.

In an essay he wrote in 1950, Chandler thought back on the pulp fiction of the decades before the War. Its "power," he proposed, lay in "the smell of fear"—a curious phrase that manages to transpose an abstract emotion into something almost physical. Probably Chandler was correct, but he may well have been describing the purgative effect of pulps on his own state of mind at the start of his career. Soon he would be writing about middle-aged detectives who, like their author, perceived themselves as isolated outsiders in a hostile world. Palpable fear was not of course peculiar to Chandler's heroes or to heroes of pulps generally. Fear as a fictional theme said something about the nature of the times as well.

Nineteen thirty-three, the year Chandler's first published short story appeared, was also a year jittery Americans were observing the spread of fascism abroad and economic depression the world over. Political movements of both the extreme right and left seemed to many to be taking root on American soil, while the violence, sadism, and ruthlessness of criminal gangs seemed all too similar to the behavior of fascists abroad. Some of the political fiction of the time, such as Sinclair Lewis's *It Can't Happen Here* and Nathaniel West's *A Cool Million* dealt with the emergence of American fascism. E. E. Cummings' *him* (1927) portrays European dictators as American gangsters; Cummings suggested that hidden homosexual elements lay behind the tough-guy veneer of his fascists and their hatred of "fairies." Neither Chandler nor Hammett portrayed their tough homosexual-baiting detectives as fascists or as being anything but masculine, but despite Hammett's and Chandler's democratic proclivities, the violent private eye who possesses little faith or patience with democratic and judicial processes has something of a vigilante mentality. (Gershon Legman in *Love and Death,* 1949, goes further and describes Chandler's Philip Marlowe as both a latent homosexual and necrophile.)

Anxiety so pervaded the nation that in his inaugural address, the new American president tried to reassure the public that the only thing they needed to fear was fear itself. Western Americans were particularly susceptible. For rootless and jobless Californians like Chandler, the sudden mass influx of Okies and other out-of-state depression victims aggravated anxieties. Hollywood meanwhile, the nation's dream factory, as Chandler once bitterly observed, continued churning out images further and further removed from the kind of life people knew.

One of the ways Americans coped with their amorphous fears was by becoming vicarious participants in what the mass circulation newspapers, magazines, and movies termed "the war against crime." In all probability the crime rate of the depression years was not much higher than in previous decades, but to an uneasy populace crime was visible, tangible, and above all comprehensible. Abolish crime, it was said, and a more secure order would be restored. Thus alert police forces or an FBI could cite "public enemies," and by picking them off, one by one, give Americans the sense that *something* was being done.

On a fantasy level, pulp detective stories also helped. By eliminating crooks and injustices (often by illegal means), the private detective in a few short pages relieved the reader of the perceived causes of his discontent. But for Chandler the pulps did not simply provide wish-fulfillment; they also served as a metaphor for the larger world. In an "Introduction" for a collection of his short stories, he commented:

> Their characters lived in a world gone wrong, a world in which long before the atom bomb, civilization had created the machinery for its own destruction and was learning to use it with all the moronic delight of a gangster trying out his first machine gun. The law was something to be manipulated for profit and power. The streets were dark with something more than night. [*Trouble is My Business* 1950]

The Depression years for Chandler were trying ones—one is tempted to say sobering, since he had evidently curtailed his drinking and begun taking his marital responsibilities seriously. It was obviously not the easiest time for a middle-aged ex-alcoholic with an English accent to pick himself up and start over. Cissy remained loyal, but the straitened circumstances of their lives required that they periodically move from one Los Angeles house to another. Perhaps Chandler's sensitivity to the mood and feel of lower middle-class life comes as much from these peregrinations as they do from his penurious youth.

He apparently determined again to try his hand at writing—or perhaps he had never given up the dream—but it is ironic that he decided to write for the lowly pulps, since one of the reasons he says he left England was that an English editor, "a suave Cantabrigian in a cutaway coat," had suggested to him that he write newspaper serials. Chandler was so affronted at "having to write what then appeared to me the most appalling garbage . . . [that] I gave him a sickly smile and left the country." Yet some twenty years later Chandler, who had evidently been studying American pulps closely— especially Hammett's work—submitted his first story, "Blackmailers Don't Shoot," to *Black Mask*. Its editor, Joseph Shaw, was so impressed that he thought him a "genius." Within the next six years Chandler would publish twenty additional stories, half of these in *Black Mask*. In most respects they followed the general formula although they clearly reveal Chandler as a cut or two above his colleagues in matters of style and character. One suspects too that for Chandler the rattling good tale existed for making some melancholy points about human nature.

Part of his melancholy may be attributed to a nostalgia for England. Time and distance had magnified her attractions, which he now evidently associated with a frustrated love affair. The bittersweet tone of Chandler's prose is prefigured in an unpublished poem written in 1932 in which he recalls England's unparalleled beauty and an unknown woman as "the promise of an impossible paradise." America, by contrast, is the "bright and dismal land of my exile and dismay." Paradoxically, the attitudes of Chandler's immediate influences, Hammett and Hemingway, may also have encouraged him in his melancholy. One does not ordinarily think of two of America's most hard-boiled authors as contributing to a third author's *langueurs,* but underneath the tough exterior exterior of their prose lay an unmistakeable *weltzschmerz* that Chandler seems to have imbibed.

Chandler drew what he needed from his contemporaries and wedded their values to his own peculiarly Victorian outlook. (Chandler wrote a rather good, but never published, parody of Hemingway at about the time he was beginning to publish his detective stories. He also names one of his typically simple-minded, tough characters in his second novel, *Farewell My Lovely,* Hemingway. The title of that book, incidentally, suggests Hemingway's own second novel, *A Farewell to Arms.*) From Hammett Chandler learned not only the main ingredients of formula but how to express a sense of resignation about ever discovering rational order in this world—a fashionable post-World War I affectation that Chandler probably never fully accepted, given his Victorian upbringing. Yet in his stories there is more than a touch of the meaninglessness of events that his detectives obsessively try to make sense of. From Hemingway he learned not only how to pare his sentences and toughen his dialogue but how to communication his heroes' private dignity in the presence of death. (Shades of Matthew Arnold and Kipling.)

The stoic behavior of Chandler's heroes—a stoicism Chandler himself was not always capable of—may say something about the displacement value of literature. One thinks, for example, of the grotesque ex-convict in Chandler's short story "Try the Girl" who after seven years' absence relentlessly but hopelessly seeks out an old girl friend who has all but forgotten him. Could Chandler have been thinking of his own long absence from the English woman he once loved? What sticks about the story is not the murder mystery that attaches itself to the con's search, but the mystery of his curious idealism, his obsessive love that causes him to kill, and yet still makes him strangely sympathetic. Indeed the moral ardor of the story is directed against one of the girl's employers who wants to keep the convict away, not in order to protect her but to use her for his own selfish ends. This, as we shall see, is a theme to which Chandler would return in subsequent works: how the rich and socially powerful use and manipulate others less strong than they, as if their humanity meant nothing.

Chandler's biographer, Frank MacShane, thinks Chandler's antagonism toward the rich stems in part from his resentment of his wealthy employer at the oil company, and we know as well that Chandler despised his snobbish Irish grandmother, upon whom both he and his mother were so dependent. The theme of emotional exploitation by the rich and socially successful was of course also a notion of F. Scott Fitzgerald with whom Chandler later felt an affinity. But Chandler's class anger was more moral than political despite the fact that he used conventional symbols of social injustice—brutal police, corrupt officials, venal lawyers, and so on. What he objected to was not so much the "system," as persons who use the system to intimidate others. Some of Chandler's characters blame society for their own moral weaknesses, but the very presence of Chandler's unsullied heroes represents a rebuke in itself.

Justice in Chandler is not so much "legal" as poetic. Bad guys often die not for their crimes but for their lust and their avarice. Conversely, some of Chandler's characters, including his detectives, literally get away with murder if the murder seems deserved ("Spanish Blood," 1935) or if the murderer is not psychologically responsible for his actions ("The Curtain," 1936). In each of these short stories, the detective's role is not simply to solve crimes, but to protect the weak and the troubled—often at his own expense— and to make sure, insofar as it is possible in an imperfect world, that justice is done.

Although Chandler would later claim that the ideal detective was a poor but honest man, this was not always the case in his own first writings. In one story ("Guns at Cyrano's," 1936) the detective's father had once "owned" the town, and in another ("Pearls Are a Nuisance," 1939), the hero takes a rather condescending view of the lower classes. As a rule, though, Chandler's early detectives emerge as undeveloped versions of Philip Marlowe, conforming both to Hammett's hardboiled archetype and to Chandler's evolving chivalric code. If their adventures tax belief, this too is partially convention. Action is primary, plausibility secondary. Chandler often extricates his detectives from sticky situations by having the bad guys kill one another off in one climactic scene. The story is told that Joseph Shaw, the editor of *Black Mask,* once advised his writers that if ever they were stymied for plot, they might have one or two thugs come through the door with guns in their hands; such persons do make occasional appearances in Chandler's apprentice fiction.

Yet Chandler's tales are so fast-paced his readers have little time to remark on their absurdities. Actions unfold in terse hard sentences characterized by simple monosyllabic words:

> Marty didn't like that. His lower lip went in under his teeth and his eyebrows drew down at the corners. His whole face got mean.
>
> The buzzer kept on buzzing.
>
> The blonde stood up quickly. Nerve tension made her face old and ugly.
>
> Watching me, Marty jerked a small drawer open in the tall desk and got a small, white-handled automatic out of it. He held it out to the blonde. She went to him and took it gingerly, not liking it.
>
> "Sit down next to the shamus," he rasped. "Hold the gun on him. If he gets funny feed him a few."
>
> The blonde sat down on the davenport about three feet from me, on the side away from the door. She lined the gun on my leg. I didn't like the jerky look in her green eyes. ["Killer in the Rain"]

Likewise gore and death are described almost clinically with few, if any, encumbering phrases that might decelerate the story.

> Braced to the door frame by eight hooked fingers, all but one of which were white as wax, there hung what was left of a man.
>
> He had eyes an eighth of an inch deep, china-blue, wide open. They looked at me but they didn't see me. He had coarse gray hair on which the smeared blood looked purple. One of his temples was a pulp, and the tracery of blood from it reached clear to the point of his chin. The one straining finger that wasn't white had been pounded to shreds as far as the second joint. Sharp splinters of

bone stuck out of the mangled flesh. Something that might once have been a fingernail looked now like a ragged splinter of glass. ["Bay City Blues"]

Lightning changes in the hero's precarious fortunes produce the principal effects of these stories—that smell of fear. Sometimes the detectives merely fear for their lives. But what Chandler seemed really to be aiming for was a larger sense of fear, an undefined malaise that hangs over events before they happen, a fear the more terrifying because, he suggests, sudden death lies as much in the familiar as in the unknown. Thus an atmosphere of threat hovers over Chandler's city streets, shabby offices, and rented rooms. By the time he came to write his first novel Chandler would be much more successful in putting all of these elements together.

The Big Sleep was published by Knopf in 1939. The following year *Farewell My Lovely* appeared. There was no question now that Chandler's star had risen. Hollywood bought both novels, the first of which would become a 1946 film classic, directed by Howard Hawks and featuring Humphrey Bogart, formerly Hammett's Sam Spade in *The Maltese Falcon*. Other books followed at longer intervals: *The High Window* (1942), *The Lady in the Lake* (1943), *The Little Sister* (1949), *The Long Goodbye* (1953), and *Playback* (1958). All but *Playback* were made into movies, most of which were produced under different titles; *Farewell My Lovely,* for example, was called *The Falcon Takes Over* (RKO, 1941) and *Murder My Sweet* (RKO, 1945).

From 1942 to 1946 Chandler wrote plot synopses and screenplays for Paramount and in 1950 he worked with the director, Alfred Hitchcock, on Patricia Highsmith's novel, *Strangers on a Train*. Suddenly, well into his fifties, he had become a celebrated figure. Yet judging from his letters and the few personal essays he wrote dealing with Hollywood, literature, and his own aspirations, he was not very uplifted by his fame. Chandler resumed drinking heavily, which on one occasion led to his being taken off an assignment. Despite his frequent complaints that Hollywood was false, corrupt, and commercial, one suspects that what he hated most was how attracted and vulnerable he was to the very tawdriness he deplored. Studio work brought him once again into close contact with young women and again he had affaris— but Cissy forgave him.

Like his predecessor, Hammett, Chandler remained a loner. After 1945 neither Cissy nor Chandler was seen about much. Cissy was said to be more self-conscious than ever about her age, and Chandler was embarrassed by a skin allergy he had developed. They made few friends, but as if to compensate, Chandler wrote numerous letters to readers, publishers, agents, and acquaintances about himself, his wife, his cat, and his work. One of his correspondents was S. J. Perelman who thought no one wrote better accounts of Southern California. In 1946 the Chandlers moved to the fashionable outlying town of La Jolla presumably to get away from the hurly-burly of Hollywood. But although the quiet new community pleased him at first, he did not especially like the rich and elderly retired people who lived there. "It's for old people and their parents," he wrote one correspondent, and to another he spoke of "arthritic billionaires and barren old women." Less than three years after the move, he told of feeling "dull and depressed . . . too often."

Chandler, as he put it, "cannibalized" his short stories to write *The Big Sleep.* Several of his other novels were written the same way: he took ideas, themes, characters, and sometimes whole passages from his pulp writing and incorporated them into his longer fiction. He did not of course imagine that anyone would ever seek out the magazine origins of these books, but if the Chandler scholar wants to discover some of his sources they are not hard to find. It should not be supposed though that Chandler's borrowings are the consequence of an arrested imagination. His novels considerably improve upon his short stories by sharpening, condensing, and meshing them. The cannibalized parts constitute only small portions of the novels and are often employed for entirely different purposes than they were in their original spots. For example, although the main plot ideas of *The Big Sleep* come from two earlier pieces, "The Curtain" (1936), and "Killer in the Rain" (1935), the solution to the mystery lies outside these stories. He changes characters as well. In *Farewell My Lovely,* a woman who was treated sympathetically in her pulp origins, "Try the Girl" (1937), reemerges in the novel as a heartless calculating killer. In fact, she too is an amalgam, derived in part from the villainess of another story, "Mandarin's Jade" (1937).

The Big Sleep opens with Philip Marlowe's summons by a General Sternwood who asks his help in exposing an unknown blackmailer. While trying to do this, Marlowe unearths several blackmailing schemes bit by bit, and in so doing discovers venality, guilt, and shame wherever he turns. To be sure, there are exceptions, including the private "soldierly" virtues of the ancient dying General Sternwood, whose values, we are given to feel, are about to die with him. The General possesses an unflinching honesty about himself and his daughters, and a towering loyalty to his son-in-law, a former fighter for Irish freedom, who has unaccountably vanished. The General's loyalty is matched by that shown by Harry Jones, a shabby, low-level crook, who remains faithful to his grasping, self-serving sweetheart. Rather than betray her, Harry dies horribly of cyanide poisoning. Finally Marlowe's own compassion for the General results in attempts to rescue reluctant ladies in distress.

As knight errant in a nonchivalric world, Marlowe saves himself from the absurdity of his role by a wry sense of humor.

> The main hallway of the Sternwood place was two stories high. Over the entrance doors, which would have let in a troop of Indian elephants, there was a broad stained-glass panel showing a knight in dark armor rescuing a lady who was tied to a tree and didn't have any clothes on but some very long and convenient hair. The knight had pushed the vizor of his helmet back to be sociable, and he was fiddling with the knots on the ropes that tied the lady to the

> tree and not getting anywhere. I stood there and thought that if I lived in the house, I would sooner or later have to climb up there and help him. He didn't seem to be really trying.

Nonetheless Marlowe takes his job seriously; from time to time we see him alone in his apartment pushing a knight across a chessboard as he muses about what to do next. At one point he describes himself as "painfully" honest in what one of the General's daughters describes as "this rotten crime-ridden country" and despite the fact that he is at constant odds with both criminals and police (most of whom are cynical, brutal, or resigned to corruption), he carries on courageously and alone. Above all he is an individualist, suspicious of all social institutions, who insists on doing "my thinking myself."

In reaction to his realization that greed and lust lie behind the crimes he investigates, Marlowe is also something of an ascetic. He scarcely makes a living at "twenty-five dollars a day and expenses" and seems to take a rather dim view of sex. He loathes "pansys" (one of whom is a murderer and another a pornographer and blackmailer), but although he claims he is as "warmblooded as the next guy," he rejects, for no discernible reason, the blandishments of the Sternwood daughters. When he finds the younger, Carmen, awaiting him naked in his bed one night, he equates her carnality with evil. "A hissing noise came tearing out of her mouth." Perhaps the key is that her presence threatens his insularity.

> I didn't mind what she called me. . . . But this was the room I had to live in. It was all I had in the way of a home. In it was everything that was mine, that had any association for me, any past, anything that took the place of a family.

He throws her out and slowly drinks a glass of whiskey, then tears "the bed to pieces savagely." Afterwards he writes, "You can have a hangover from other things than alcohol. I had one from women. Women made me sick."

Men and women rarely respect one another in Chandler's works. At best they make tenuous and temporary alliances for what they regard as mutual gain—but betrayal is always imminent. In *The Big Sleep* the only true positive relationship is the one that existed between the General and his vanished son-in-law, for whom Marlowe, in a sense, becomes the substitute. Not until *The Long Goodbye* (1953) would Chandler again allow his hero to express such intense feelings toward other human beings.

In retrospect we begin to suspect that much of the terror that lies at the root of Chandler's novels and makes his tough guys *act* tough is a morbid fear of sexuality. For example, Carmen, whose name suggests Bizet's femme fatale, is described as having "predatory teeth." Even the vegetation in the General's hothouse possesses a kind of moribund carnality: "The glass walls and roof were heavily misted and big drops of moisture splashed down on the plants. . . . The plants filled the place, a forest of them, with nasty meaty leaves and stalks like the newly washed fingers of dead men." In an image reminiscent of Eliot's "Prufrock," Marlowe writes: "Under the thinning fog the surf curled and creamed, almost without sound, like a thought trying to form itself on the edge of consciousness." Indeed even when Chandler's imagery is less explicitly sensual, danger lurks everywhere in the vibrancy of nature, however much men may attempt to domesticate it: "[The] bright gardens had a haunted look, as though small wild eyes were watching me from behind bushes, as though the sunshine itself had a mysterious something in its light."

For Chandler, the tangible and real portend the mysterious, and the familiar often betokens fear of the unknown. A typical passage in *The Big Sleep* begins: "It was a wide room the whole width of the house. It had a low beamed ceiling and brown plaster walls decked out with strips of Chinese embroidery and Chinese and Japanese prints in grand wood frames." Five sentences follow, each beginning with "There" or "There were," listing the contents of the room, its furnishings, its color and the odd paraphernalia scattered about in it. The last sentence, however, shifts swiftly from the visual to the olefactory implying violence, death, and perversity.

> The room contained an odd assortment of odors, of which the most emphatic at the moment seemed to be the pungent aftermath of cordite and the sickish aroma of ether.

At his best, Chandler was surely one of the masters of the American language. Events in *The Big Sleep* are recounted with great economy, and suspense and atmosphere are fused into what might best be termed Los Angeles gothic. Here and there, he will follow pulp conventions and torture a simile: An empty house is "as dismal as a lost dog"; a woman's hat "looked as if you could have made it with one hand out of a dark blotter" and people who patronize pornography shops are "as nervous as a dowager who can't find the rest room." But he is a master at using dialogue to identify both social class and character. Eddie Mars sardonically addresses Marlowe as "soldier"—which he is, in a manner of speaking. And here is Harry Jones, "a three for a quarter grifter" who wants to sell Marlowe information about the General's son-in-law.

> I knew Rusty myself. Not well, well enough to say "How's a boy?" and he'd answer me or he wouldn't, according to how he felt. A nice guy though. I always liked him. . . . High strung. Rusty wouldn't get along with [his rich wife]. But Jesus, he'd get along with her old man's dough, wouldn't he? That's what you think. This Regan was a cockeyed sort of buzzard. He had long-range eyes. He was looking over into the next valley all the time. He wasn't scarcely around where he was.

Chandler's second book, *Farewell, My Lovely* (1940), was even more popular than his first. Created in part from cannibalizations of his earlier story "Try the Girl," *Farewell* deals with Marlowe's pursuit of an ex-con who is searching for his former sweetheart. In the course of his quest, the con, a giant named Moose Malloy, kills the manager of a Negro social club and Marlowe promises to help a demoralized detective lieutenant find him. Nulty, the lieutenant, complains to Marlowe that nobody in the police or newspapers really cares about "shine killings." In some respects the novel is more of a social statement than Chandler's first. A crooked cop tells Marlowe: "Cops don't get crooked for money. . . . They get caught in the system. . . . You gotta play the game dirty or you don't eat." His suggestion for making the world over, however, is Moral Rearmament.

Marlowe's adventures lead him from the very bottom to the top strata of Los Angeles society, whose foibles he denounces in acid tones. He visits the eerie home of a fashionable Southern California "psychic consultant" (not unlike the one in which Hammett's Op found himself in *The Dain Curse*), and a sanatorium that is really a hideout for wanted criminals. In both of these, Marlowe is taken prisoner and given the ritual beating that private detectives must take before they are allowed to carry on.

Nearly everyone he meets, regardless of social class, is hardened and corrupt, but the streets and houses of lower middle class neighborhoods may also convey the resignation and despair of their inhabitants.

> 1644 West 54th Place was a dried-out house with a dried-out brown lawn in front of it. There was a large bare patch around a tough-looking palm tree. On the porch stood one lonely wooden rocker, and the afternoon breeze made the unpruned shoots of last year's poinsettias tap-tap against the cracked stucco walls. A line of stiff yellowish half-washed clothes jittered on a rusty wire in the side yard.

The moneyed classes on the other hand link themselves to criminals when they feel it is to their advantage, and buy and sell politicians and the police; yet despite their power, they are almost as fearful and unhappy as anyone else. And because they believe in nothing, they clutch desparately at anything to secure their precarious identities. Here in splendid Americanese, Marlowe speaks of the unhappy rich who consult Jules Amthor, the Charlatan psychic consultant.

> Give him enough time and pay him enough money and he'll cure anything from a jaded husband to a grasshopper plague. He would be an expert in frustrated love affairs, women who slept alone and didn't like it, wandering boys and girls who didn't write home, sell the property now or hold it for another year, will this part hurt me with my public or make me seem more versatile. . . . A fakeloo artist, a hoopla spreader, and a lad who had his card rolled up inside sticks of tea, found on a dead man.

In his fashion Chandler had declared Southern California to be as much a spiritual wasteland as Eliot's London.

Marlowe feels self-disgust on more than one occasion when he is forced to do disagreeable things in the line of duty. At one point he plies an alcoholic widow with liquor to glean more information from her, and at another feels as "nasty" as if "he had picked a poor man's pocket," when he is discovered by a Mr. Grayle just as he is about to kiss the elderly gentleman's wife. He knows he is not all that good at his job; at one point, he is hired as a bodyguard, only to have his client murdered in his presence.

Still, it is not all self-hatred. Earlier on in the book he describes a "smeary self portrait" of Rembrandt on a calendar. Marlowe might well have been describing himself. The "face was aging, saggy, fully of the disgust of life and the thickening effects of liquor. But it had a hard cheerfulness . . . and the eyes were as bright as dew." And indeed Marlowe displays a certain zest for life and is not always so moralistic towards his antagonists. Several of his exchanges with Nulty are truly funny and he expresses some sympathy for the isolated, love-lorn, and grotesque, even when they kill. Perhaps this was because he was beginning to feel a kinship with them.

Chandler's books of the war decade are something of a mixed bag. In two of them he appears to be taking himself overseriously while at the same time making fun of himself. *The High Window* (1942) and *The Little Sister* (1949) were probably intended partially as self-parodies and partially as hints of Chandler's mixed feelings about himself both as an artist and as a commercial success. By poking fun at himself, Chandler seems to be saying: "You see, I don't take this sort of writing as anything more than a bit of fun." But segments of these novels are tense, suspenseful, and moralistic, as if Chandler were somehow afraid to commit himself entirely to satire for fear of losing his mass audience.

The High Window is probably the best of his post-*Farewell* books of the 1940s. (Chandler thought it his worst.) It begins almost as a parody of *The Big Sleep* with Marlowe calling on a rich, crotchety, domineering, old woman who in certain respects is the female counterpart of General Sternwood. She wants him to track down a rare coin she believes stolen from her collection. Here, Marlowe does not identify himself with a knight, as he did in *The Big Sleep*, but with an absurd painted statue of a Negro on the lawn, dressed in riding gear, and wearing a sad, discouraged expression on his face as if he had been waiting too long. On the block at his feet, there is an iron hitching ring. Marlowe pats the Negro on the head and says, "You and me both, brother."

There are one or two other passages that imply Marlowe's social consciousness; one is a description of a rundown outlying town called Bunker Hill (an ironic allusion to America's revolutionary glory?). Marlowe tells of its declining neighborhoods and streets, the flyblown restaurants, the rooming houses with their lost and desperate inhabitants:

> In the tall rooms, haggard landladies bicker with shifty tenants. On the wide cool front porches, reaching their cracked shoes into the sun, and staring at nothing, sit the old men with faces like lost battles.

A verb or a phrase may say all. Somewhere "a radio is blatting a ball game." In an alley stand "four tall battered garbage pails in a line with a dance of flies in the sunlit air above them."

These images have the feel of Eliot's "Preludes" or passages from "Prufrock," but the novel as a whole hearkens back to Chandler's Fitzgeraldian theme of how the rich and powerful use those less fortunate than they. In contrast to the present-day exploitative West Coast, Chandler has a vision of a simpler, more honest America that existed in the past and perhaps lives on still in the Midwest. As the novel ends, the chivalrous Marlowe takes the depleted heroine back to her Kansas home for spiritual and emotional renewal, not unlike the narrator of *Gatsby* who plans to return to his Midwestern home for the same reasons.

The plot and characters in *The High Window* are artificial; on one occasion Marlowe complains that everyone he meets behaves as if he were playing a role in a B movie. In places, the novel pokes fun at elite critics who derided Chandler's stuff, as when Marlowe tells a startled customer in a drugstore whom he thinks is "sneering" at him over a copy of the *New Republic*, "You ought to lay off that fluff and get into something solid, like a pulp magazine." Walking away, he hears someone say, "Hollywood's full of them."

Chandler's next book, *The Lady in the Lake* (1943), represents a departure of sorts from his earlier work. Much of the action takes place not in the city but in the mountains east of Los Angeles, and here Chandler moves from the argot of the streets to a stylized version of rural speech. There are no extremes of wealth and poverty, nor are there professional gangsters. Possibly America's mood of wartime unity dictated playing down class differences and the menace of organized crime.

The Little Sister (1949) was published six years later but nonetheless looks like a hurry-up job. It appeared after Chandler had for the most part given up studio work and was probably intended as a "Hollywood novel." There are several lively depictions of Hollywood types—talent agents and their hacks, unemployed actors, and so on. There is a wonderful scene on a Hollywood lot where Marlowe meets a film mogul whose incontinent boxer dogs pee and root about while the mogul complains to Marlowe that everyone in the movie business is up to his neck in sex, and the more mistakes one makes, the more money one gets. Chandler reverses many of his earlier themes. The "bad guys" come from the "pure" Midwest to exploit and extort money from a Hollywood movie actress. The seemingly naive heroine who supplicates Marlowe for help is really a ruthless blackmailer, the police are sometimes sympathetic, and the rich and powerful seem sometimes quite bewildered.

But as a whole, *Little Sister* is really not much of an achievement, lying somewhere between intended and, one suspects, unintended burlesque. Hotblooded females throw themselves at the impervious Marlowe who meditates unhappily about soul-destroying materialism. Perhaps by now the times had passed Chandler by. The war was over and machismo and the stiff upper lip—that nice blend of very English and very American stoicism that

Chandler brought to his earlier writings—no longer seemed applicable. In some ways he may have sensed this.

The last ten years of Chandler's life are a sad mix of success and degradation. These were years in which he would write his most ambitious and perhaps interesting book, *The Long Goodbye* (1954), and his most uneven, *Playback* (1958). They were years in which he made several triumphant returns to England (the first with Cissy) but responded to his welcome with ambivalence. In the 1940s he had had a large following in England, both among intellectuals and less educated readers—his last three books were published first in England—but on his visits he feared the admiration was condescending and reacted irritably. Possibly he was responding to the snubs he had received in his youth or perhaps he himself deeply felt, despite his protestations to the contrary, that mystery writing was not quite respectable. In any case his reactions were a source of puzzlement to his hosts who for the most part were Chandler aficionados like Stephen and Natasha Spender, Ian Fleming, and J. B. Priestly.

In 1954 Cissy, now in her eighties, died of fibrosis of the lungs. Chandler was beside himself with grief. Several times he called friends and threatened suicide—and once indeed shot off a gun in his bathtub, probably by accident. He had begun drinking heavily again, so heavily in fact that on a number of occasions he required hospitalization. When he was not drinking, he often seemed to be playing out the dreams he had hitherto confined to his writing. From time to time he assumed the Philip Marlowe role of protector and defender of helpless women. As a consequence he sometimes found himself in peculiar situations. At one point he almost married a fan who had written to him, and at another, he made his troubled Australian secretary the beneficiary of his will. He evidently thought better of both intentions later.

In his five remaining years Chandler made a number of other trips to England. His behavior in England was not much different from what it had been in California. His friends write that he liked to think of himself as enormously attractive to the young English women to whom he was introduced, although there is very little evidence that he was. One of the women who took him seriously was Helga Greene, a literary agent. Helga probably had few illusions about him, but after several years of spotty courtship she agreed to marry him.

In March of 1959 Chandler entrained to California from New York where he had just been inaugurated president of the Mystery Writers of America. Later he planned to rejoin Helga in London. On the way, he fell ill with pneumonia. Once more he began to drink, and once more he was taken from his La Jolla quarters for hospitalization. Several days later he died. Seventeen people attended his funeral. Scarcely any of them had more than a passing acquaintance with the deceased.

Although Chandler planned periodically to do nondetective fiction, nothing much came of it. If one can read between the lines of his letters and essays, he probably felt that the conventions of tough-guy fiction did not leave him sufficient leeway to develop character, although he may have realized, in a deeper sense, that the genre imposed retraints on his latent sentimentality. Still, he was unhappy and in his next-to-last novel, *The Long Goodbye* (1953), we find him bending the genre to what he must have regarded as the freer spaces of the traditional novel. It was something of a try at having one's cake and eating it.

The plot of the novel is as complicated and contrived as anything Chandler had written. In part it deals with Marlowe's arbitrary friendship with a besotted young man, Terry Lennox, who later pretends to have committed suicide. Marlowe feels bitter about his friend's deception, but the reader may think Marlowe's reaction excessive in view of the fact that Terry had been fleeing the police. The novel contains Chandler's usual quota of phony psychiatrists, rotten cops, nasty gangsters, and corrupt millionaires, but more significant are Marlowe's relationships with the suicidal alcoholic hack writer, Roger Wade, his beautiful and seductive suicidal wife Eileen, and Terry's beautiful and seductive sister-in-law, Linda Loring. Marlowe suffers another brutal beating at the hands of the cops (this time on Terry's behalf) before certain murders are accounted for.

Marlowe's hardboiled exterior—and perhaps Chandler's as well—is pierced to a greater extent in this novel than in previous works. The first thing that strikes the reader is the number of suicides or pretended suicides in the novel, as if Chandler were anticipating his own suicide attempts after Cissy's death. One also notices Marlowe's attachment to two alcoholic men, Terry and Roger, the latter being an author of popular books who hates himself because he has not lived up to his artistic possibilities; Terry and Roger are evidently Chandler-Marlowe's alter egos. Finally, the novel serves as a vehicle for Chandler's extended comments on society, justice, democracy, private and public morality, the responsibilities of friends, lovers, and artists, not to mention blondes and Mexicans.

The main business of the novel is not with the crimes Marlowe resolves to uncover—although that is its pretense—but with the issue of male friendship and its betrayal. (Marlowe's confrontations with the women, Linda and Eileen, are less intense though sexual and sentimentalized.) When Terry turns up alive at the end of the novel, Marlowe learns he has played dead at the behest of certain gangsters and his crooked millionaire father-in-law. Worse still, Marlowe, equating moral with sexual perversity, suggests that Terry has become a homosexual and severs his friendship with him. Considering Marlowe's general dislike of homosexuals in this and other books, one wonders whether what he feared most was his desire for closeness with other men. Was his author suppressing a longing for the father he never had?

Marlowe's relationship with the hack writer, Wade, is less personal. Part of Wade's misery is caused by his mistaken belief that he killed Terry's wife in a fit of alcoholic passion, but the larger cause of his wretchedness is that he has never fully realized himself as an author and has sold himself out to commerce. Marlowe accuses him of wallowing in self-pity—an accusation that might just as easily be leveled at both Marlowe and his creator. Throughout the novel, Marlowe complains again and again that he is tired, sick, and disgusted and wonders how and why he ever got into the private eye business. He seems to have lost much of his zest for life.

In part Marlowe's weary tones are tied to his fierce contempt for the upper classes. Both Marlowe and Terry speak at length about the tedium and sterility of the lives of the rich, their homes, their communities, their carelessness about other people, and their capacities to corrupt political and judicial processes. This constant barrage is surprising in that it was written at a time (the early 1950s) when Chandler was himself fairly well off and the political climate of the country was conservative. Chandler may have been venting his disgust at the dreary rich he had been living among in La Jolla. Like F. Scott Fitzgerald, whom he had long admired, Chandler looked at the moneyed classes with both envy and revulsion.

We have noted Fitzgeraldian elements in some of Chandler's other works but the parallels are most striking in *Goodbye.* For one thing Wade, the drunken writer, alludes to himself as another F. Scott Fitzgerald. But beyond this, there are other correspondences with *The Great Gatsby,* as Leon Howard argues in his essay, "Raymond Chandler's Not-So-Great Gatsby (*Mystery & Detection Annual,* 1973). Terry Lennox, like Gatsby, is a returned soldier who discovers that the woman whom he had idealized is now married to another. Both Terry and Gatsby have criminal connections and Eileen Wade, like Daisy, kills her husband's mistress after which Terry, like Gatsby, takes the blame. But where Fitzgerald celebrates Gatsby's capacity to dream, Chandler, the stricter moralist, condemns Terry to a life of banishment and homosexuality.

Still, Chandler's morality does not prevent Marlowe from having one brief sexual liaison with a married woman. To be sure, Linda Loring is the wife of a prig and we are given to believe her marriage will soon end. She is, however, exceedingly rich and therefore, according to Marlowe's principles, too careless and too irresponsible for any kind of permanent relationship. Marlowe's rejection of her is not unlike Nick Carroway's rejection of Jordan Baker in *The Great Gatsby.* But the mere fact that he surrenders himself for even a short time announces some kind of breakdown of the hardboiled code.

If Marlowe engages in a brief sexual liaison in *The Long Goodbye,* he is an absolute wanton four years later in Chandler's last novel, *Playback* (1958). Not only does he make love to the heroine, but he also sleeps with the secretary of one of his clients. In the latter case the sex is quite gratuitous, having nothing to do with the plot or anything else in the novel except perhaps Marlowe's ego. Both women think he is terrific.

Playback is not so bad a novel as some of Chandler's critics contend. For one thing, the author returns to the sort of situation he handles best—the rescue of a lovely lady in distress. The setting is now no longer Los Angeles but an insular suburban La Jolla-type town called Esmeralda whose history, values, and prejudices Chandler depicts wickedly as he tells his story with vitality and wit. The basic plot ideas were originally intended as a screen play which Chandler had to change drastically in order to put into narrative form. While the novel does not add much to Chandler's reputation, there are some passages as good as any he had ever written.

Before his death, Chandler undertook two other Marlowe projects, including an unfinished novel, *Poodle Springs,* in which Marlowe is married to the rich Linda Loring of *Goodbye.* Their prospects are not promising; Marlowe with his spartan ways and Linda with her sybarite notions look as if they are about to clash. Chandler also wrote a short story, his first in twenty-three years, in which Marlowe attempts to defend a Mafia gangster from other Mafia gangsters who have been contracted to kill him. It was, as Chandler said, a good idea but the story did not quite jell. In his lifetime Chandler produced a few nondetective pieces. In them, we might again note Chandler's attempts to marry fantasy or romance to what he regarded as the sad and sordid exigencies of the real world. Some have been published posthumously more for the light they throw on Chandler than for their intrinsic literary merit. None need detain us here.

How do we account for the continuing popularity of Chandler with his present-day audience? Several possibilities suggest themselves. He was a superb storyteller, and while we may occasionally be amused at Marlowe's tough sentimentality, more significantly we are drawn to Marlowe because he is decisive and self-possessed in a perplexing, threatening, indifferent world. In some ways it is a world not unlike our own, fraught with tensions, terror, wars, and economic crisis. As Chandler observed in his famous essay, "The Simple Art of Murder" (1944), his hero is a poor man, unafraid of "mean streets," and above all "a man of honor." Thus, unlike the antiheroes or "survivors" of contemporary letters, Marlowe carries forward the tradition of the true democratic hero, the uncommon commoner, certain of his values.

It is thus clear that Marlowe would not have had very much sympathy for Sam Spade's startling perception of a world without meaning, although on several occasions Marlowe himself very nearly succumbs to despair. Near the end of *Playback* Marlowe says of himself: "Wherever I went, whatever I did, this is what I would come back to. A blank wall in a meaningless room in a meaningless house." Fortunately a phone call from Linda Loring lifts him from his despondency, but a better answer arrives earlier in the novel when Marlowe meets an old man in a hotel lobby wearing gloves (as Chandler did) because "my hands are ugly and painful." The old man refuses to despair and suggests to Marlowe that meaning may derive from the very nature of one's struggle to discover meaning. Surely this is what Chandler would have liked to believe. Possibly this is what his books are really about.

> How strange it is that man's aspirations, dirty little animal that he is, his finest actions also, his great and unselfish heroism, his constant daily courage in a harsh world—how strange that these things should be so much greater than his fate on earth. That has to be somehow made reasonable. Don't tell me that honor is merely a chemical reaction or that a man who deliberately gives his life

for another is merely following a behavior pattern. Is God happy with the poisoned cat dying alone by convulsions behind the billboard? . . . There is no success where there is no possibility of failure, no art without the resistance of the medium. Is it blasphemy to suggest that God has his bad days when nothing goes right, and that God's days are very, very long?

Elliott Gould and
Mark Rydell in
The Long Goodbye by
Raymond Chandler
(*courtesy United Artists*)

Raymond Chandler
(*courtesy Alfred A. Knopf*)

Humphrey Bogart, Peter Lorre, Mary Astor, and Sydney Greenstreet as they appeared in *The Maltese Falcon* by Dashiell Hammett (*courtesy Warner Brothers, Inc.*)

Dashiell Hammett (*courtesy UPI*)

Godfrey Cambridge and
Raymond St. Jacques in
Cotton Comes To Harlem
by Chester Himes
(*courtesy United Artists*)

Chester Himes (*courtesy
Doubleday & Co., Inc.*)

Ross Macdonald
(Hans Albers–Globe Photos, Inc.)

Joanne Woodward and Paul Newman
in *The Drowning Pool* by
Ross Macdonald
(courtesy Warner Brothers, Inc.)

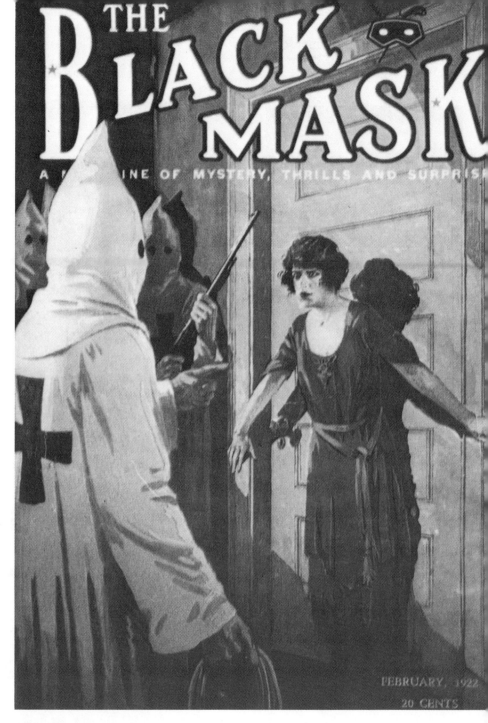

Black Mask, the first magazine to
devote itself exclusively to hardboiled
detectives. Hammett and Chandler
were early, and later famous,
contributors, while both Himes and
Macdonald were avid readers.

Another example of a pulp thriller of the Depression era.

A 1905 *Nick Carter Weekly*. Created by John R. Coryell in 1881, Nick Carter was one of the earliest private eyes and by 1900 had appeared in over 1500 novels by at least fifteen different authors.

J. Edgar Hoover encouraged the transformation of his G-men into heroes in the 1930s—in turn, some of his agents may have modeled themselves on their fictional counterparts.

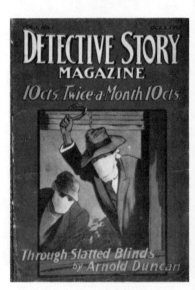

Detective Story, founded in 1915, was the first pulp, aside from the *Nick Carters*, dedicated to detective fiction.

CHAPTER 4

Chester Himes's Black Comedy: The Genre Is the Message

When the black expatriate author, Chester Himes, submitted his first police novels to his French publisher in 1957, he was not immediately aware that his two hot-tempered, fortyish, Harlem plainclothesmen were in any essential way different from the ordinary hardboiled breed. To be sure Coffin Ed Johnson and Grave Digger Jones were nominally cops, good family men with homes in Queens. But this fits the demands of the setting, for who in Harlem would have been able to afford private eyes, and besides, readers would never get to see them at home with their families. In most other respects they looked like old-fashioned independent operatives of the Hammett-Chandler variety. After the postwar decline of the pulps, tough, quirky, individualistic dicks were becoming less fashionable; still Grave Digger and Coffin Ed carried on in the old tradition doing what *they* thought was right. They often acted outside the law, manhandling suspects and criminals, and they usually found themselves free to pursue their prey without too much interference from their police bosses.

But Coffin Ed and Grave Digger made their literary debuts at a critical period when civil rights and black nationalist movements were underway. They were torn, almost from the start, between their desire to protect Harlem's exploited citizenry and their feelings that the white power structure for whom they worked was the real enemy. Like most other popular heroes, they entertained a healthy distrust of organized society, but their aroused black consciousness added new elements to their uneasiness. The rift in their loyalties would become more and more pronounced in each succeeding book until finally they were unable to perform.

Himes seems to have viewed the pulps as reflecting certain basic truths about his mother country and rather than attempt to avoid the outmoded conventions of the hardboiled formula, he employed the tough-guy genre to record his own political, social, and racial perceptions. And by the time he wrote his last novel, he had transformed the genre into an expression of the absurdities of American society. Indeed, he came to believe that absurdity was the central principle of black life.

Himes's reputation as a novelist—black, American, or expatriate—is something of a curiosity. Oddly, a number of European reviewers have the impression that Himes's detective thrillers are immensely popular in the United States. This is especially ironic in view of the fact that with the exception of his last novel, *Blind Man With A Pistol* (1969), all have received far more attention in France.

Although in France he is frequently cited in the same breath as Dashiell Hammett and Raymond Chandler, Himes's slight American recognition rests on an early protest novel (*If He Hollers Let Him Go*, 1945) and a commercially successful sex potboiler (*Pinktoes*, 1965). For his part, Himes long regarded his intervening "serious" novels as his best work—*Lonely Crusade*, 1947; *Cast The First Stone*, 1952; *The Third Generation*, 1954; and *The Primitive*, 1955—and while these received some favorable attention at their time of publication, they are now for the most part forgotten by American audiences. Moreover, his work is not even welcomed by some black American critics, who have castigated Himes for portraying Harlem in so malevolent a light; indeed, there is little likelihood that Himes will ever be accused of idealizing Harlem. Upon his return to Paris after a brief visit to the United States in 1962, he wrote a piece for *Présence Africaine* called "Harlem ou le Cancer de l'Amérique." Yet the Harlem of Himes's essay, like the Harlem of his detective fiction, is best seen as a state of mind, where the comic horror of the black experience in America is intensified and becomes visible.

Himes's admittedly autobiographical novels may provide more reliable accounts of the life and attitudes that shape his thrillers than either his interviews or his two volumes of memoirs, *The Quality of Hurt* (1972), and *My Life of Absurdity* (1976). The latter pass too quickly over important events (like his seven years in prison, and his personal and literary relationships to writers like Louis Bromfield and Ralph Ellison) and dwell often inordinately on such less significant matters as his pets, his cars, and his casual sexual encounters. His fiction is more revealing. *The Third Generation* tells of his childhood and youth, and some of his later prison years are described in more disguised fashion in *Cast The First Stone*, while *The Primitive* depicts him as a "failed" black novelist in his early forties just prior to his departure for Europe.

Himes was born in Jefferson City, Missouri in 1909, the youngest of three sons. His father, Joseph Sr.—whom he describes in *The Quality of Hurt* as short and very black, with bowed legs and an ellipsoidal skull—taught metal trades, blacksmithing and wheelwrighting at southern Negro technical colleges. Himes does not, as a rule, portray him in a flattering light. His memoirs describe him as having inherited a slave mentality "which accepts the premise that white people knew best." Joseph's marriage to Himes's mother, née Estelle Bomar, a light-complexioned woman, was unhappy, but being a teacher he was regarded as rather a success in small Southern Negro communities. It was only after the family moved North during Himes's adolescence that Joseph Sr. experienced a shattering of his self-respect.

According to Himes, his mother had long felt she had married beneath her station—in part because her husband was so much darker than she and in part, presumably, because of his docility when white people were about. She felt, moreover, that Negro colleges were rather demeaning. These views apparently made it difficult for her husband to stay on very long at any one job. They quarreled frequently and Himes says he secretly sided with her. In *The Third Generation,* Charles Taylor, Himes's fictional alter ego, "would crawl to the head of the stairs and crouch, trembling in rage and fear. He didn't hate his father. But when his parents quarreled he wanted to cut off his father's head with the chopping axe."

Not all of Himes's reminiscences of his father are hostile. From time to time he endows him with a measure of dignity and emotional balance, especially in contrast to some of his mother's excesses. It was probably more from her than from Joseph Sr. that Himes derives his conflicting racial attitudes. "My mother," he writes, ". . . liked white and felt she should have been white." She was "the complete opposite" of her husband and "hated all manner of condescension from white people." Enormously proud of the white ancestors in her background, she once wrote a book listing their names. And when her children were small, she was so fearful that they would look like Negroes that she would squeeze "the bridges of our noses to keep them from becoming flat." Little wonder that Himes would later write in *The Quality of Hurt* that blacks were not "particularly likeable" and that he found "it very difficult to like American blacks myself." He is of course not always consistent. In *My Life of Absurdity*, he says the opposite: "The only thing that kept me from being a racist was that I loved black people, felt sorry for them, which meant I was sorry for myself." Some of this same ambivalence is found in the portrayal of Himes's black detectives who express both fury at, and admiration for, their hard-pressed Harlem brethren.

Estelle Himes also attempted to instill in her children a love of music, literature, and culture. Her efforts bore fruit, for if Himes and his brothers rebelled as adolescents, each in his own way made his mark in the world: Himes's brother, Joseph Jr., became a well-known sociologist at the University of North Carolina and his oldest brother, Edward, became an official in the waiters' union in New York City. But her concern also became a problem. In *The Third Generation,* Himes tells how his fictional mother, Lillian Taylor, lavished so much love on him that he would from time to time erupt in hysterics. He clearly wanted to free himself of her smothering possessive ways, while at the same time he would be furious at himself for desiring her. Himes carried some of these attitudes into his adult years. In his memoirs, as well as in his novels, he tells of alternately tender and turbulent relationships with women (mainly white), and in his detective books he portrays a number of very strong-willed, seductive women who are threatening if not murderous to their male companions. As a popular novelist, Himes was, of course, working within the Hammett-Chandler tradition of treating beautiful women as troublemakers, but here tradition seems to have suited Himes's psychology and outlook.

The constant bickering of Himes's parents and his identification with one or the other of them at different times aroused in him feelings of guilt. Lillian Taylor in *The Third Generation* imbues her sons with a fear of an all-scrutinizing, vindictive God, and when Himes describes his protagonist's numerous near-fatal accidents, one wonders whether they may not have been self-induced as a kind of expiation. To this day Himes continues to berate himself for an accident which very nearly blinded his brother, Joseph, who in his own way, was Himes's father surrogate. He and Joseph had been preparing a high school chemistry demonstration when an explosion occurred which critically impaired Joseph's vision. (In the first of Himes's thrillers, *For Love of Imabelle,* Grave Digger Jones is also very nearly blinded when a criminal throws acid in his face.) One cannot be too sure how responsible Himes really was, but in *The Third Generation* his protagonist is made to feel guilty after the accident because earlier he had blasphemed God. The family moves North in order to find better treatment for Will Jr., Joseph Jr.'s fictional name. But northern racism and the ghetto atmosphere of St. Louis and Cleveland aggravate the parents' differences and Fess Taylor, the father, is reduced to seeking menial jobs. The disoriented children drift away from home, and mother and father are ultimately divorced. At the close of the novel, Charles traces all their misfortunes to Will's accident and as a consequence blames himself for the disintegration of the family.

Himes's adolescent years in Cleveland were fraught with more self-torment. He adopted coarse and superficial friends in the Negro bourgeois community and afterwards befriended peripheral elements of the Negro underworld in the black slums. Later on, as a first-year student at Ohio State University he was suspended for taking other students to the Negro ghetto to visit prostitutes, an activity he had been indulging in himself for some time. Meanwhile he had begun a career of crime, at first associating with professional gamblers (the name of one of whom, Bunch Boy, reappears as that of a numbers racketeer in his 1960 novel, *All Shot Up*), and then pimping, bootlegging, stealing cars and weapons, and forging checks. Finally he tried armed robbery, was apprehended, and though only nineteen, sentenced to twenty years in the Ohio State Penitentiary.

It is hard to see politically radical roots in Himes's aberrant behavior. He says in his autobiography that he dreamed of going "somewhere where . . . black people weren't the shit of the earth." But at this time, his dreams of racial escape took on distinctive bourgeois coloring. He planned to flee to Mexico with the proceeds of his robbery and live there like any affluent sybarite. It would seem that his crimes were less a rebellion against society, than they were cockeyed attempts to attain or at least conform to certain middle-class images of success—images he may have gleaned in part from his university milieu. While at Ohio State he had joined a Negro fraternity, drove fast cars, and wore a raccoon coat. As late as 1947 he recognized he still remained attached to white middle-class notions of success. "As I look back now," he wrote Carl Van Vechten, "I feel that much of my retardation as a writer has been due to a [subconscious] and conscious and deliberate desire to escape my past. All mixed up no doubt with the Negro's desire for respectability. It brought a lot of confusion to my mind. . . ."

The desire for respectability may to a certain extent explain the adolescent Himes's shock and bitterness at the severity of his prison sentence. He may have felt that white society had punished him for playing the middle class game. Today Himes, who has since adopted revolutionary and black nationalist principles, often sounds angrier than many of his proletarian colleagues. Perhaps this has something to do with his own unmet expectations of success. Racism often rankles the middle class more than the poor who have fewer hopes to begin with.

Long before his incarceration Himes had begun thinking about divine responsibility for life's injustices. After the explosion that took his brother's vision, Charles, in *The Third Generation*, thinks bitterly, "God didn't even know the difference" between right and wrong, for it was Charles who should have been punished. Indeed the title, *The Third Generation*, contains an ironic Biblical allusion to the sins of the fathers—in Himes's case, slaves!—being visited on their children and their children's children. Himes's ironic attitude toward religion is also reflected in his detective stories where religious messages are constantly being used to delude black humanity. But, curiously, many of Himes's characters possess something akin to religious fervor themselves, however antisocial their behavior. There is a driven quality about them, as if their lives are beyond their control and they must behave as they do regardless of consequences. Crooks relentlessly seek elusive fortunes that they know will destroy them, innocents persistently pursue women who have betrayed them and will do so again, and even Coffin Ed and Grave Digger risk their lives far beyond the call of duty. The wounds they incur for causes they no longer believe in defy rational explanation.

One can see then why the hardboiled genre with its emphasis on action rather than plausible motive would appeal to Himes. There was something compulsive about his own behavior as well as about the behavior of others he knew. Nothing can be more illustrative of this than Himes's several accounts of his own capture and arrest after the crime that would send him to the penitentiary. He writes that he attempted to sell his loot to a well-known pawnbroker. But the broker went into a back room on some pretext and Himes knew instinctively that he was calling the police. Himes says that he could easily have fled but did not. He was unable to move. In two of his short stories of the 1930s and in his prison novel, *Cast the First Stone*, he comes back again and again to these frozen moments. What caused his paralysis? Was it courage or fear—or an overactive conscience asking for punishment?

Himes spent seven and a half years in prison and was paroled in 1936.

These years provided him with a gold mine of material for his later detective books. Many of the stories told him by convicts and guards return in one way or another in his fiction. It was in prison too that he decided to become a writer. Possibly he thought of it as a way of acquiring an identity that would win him respect. In *The Quality of Hurt* he says that convicts looked with awe at anyone who could use a typewriter, and in one of his first short stories he tells of a convict who wrote because he wanted "others to see his name." To a certain extent he succeeded. His first pieces appeared in 1929 in the *Pittsburgh Courier* and later he turned to other Negro publications. By 1934 *Esquire* had begun printing his short prison fiction, putting him in the company of such august white authors as Hemingway, Fitzgerald, Dos Passos, and Ring Lardner. What may be more important is that Himes found he need not totally despair of his criminal past and incarceration. At least there was material here for literature—something he would remember in the late 1950s when his situation once again seemed precarious. His prison years may even have been liberating since, despite humiliations and cruelties, he arrived at a sense of himself apart from his parents.

Emotional survival was not the only challenge of prison life. Himes lived through one of the worst fires in prison history when on Easter Monday, 1930, much of the Ohio State Penitentiary went up in flames, and more than three hundred convicts died. Himes describes the holocaust in grisly detail in his first *Esquire* story, "To A Red Hell" (1934), and again years later in his 1952 novel, *Cast The First Stone*. The latter work, significantly, deals with a young convict's growth to maturity as a consequence of adversity. And Himes reiterates the strengths he gained in prison in *The Quality of Hurt*:

> I grew to manhood in the Ohio State Penitentiary. I was nineteen years old when I went in and twenty-six years old when I came out. I became a man, dependent on no one but myself. I learned all the behavior patterns necessary for survival, or I wouldn't have survived, although at the time I did not realize I was learning them.

He learned whatever he had to learn well, for survival—physical, mental, and emotional—continues as a central theme in all of Himes's work.

None of Himes's first *Esquire* stories contains identifiable black characters. Presumably Himes and his *Esquire* editors implicitly agreed that white readers would not be interested in stories written by a Negro author. Such pandering to prejudice probably seemed senseless to Himes but by now very little could have surprised him. Prison life—especially the violence of prison life—had reconfirmed his sense of the absurd. In the first volume of his memoirs he tells how convicts stabbed, cut, slashed, brained, maimed, and killed each other for the most nonsensical reasons. "Two black convicts cut each other to death over a dispute as to whether Paris was in France or France in Paris." (Grave Digger tells the same story about two blacks to an Irish police lieutenant in *The Crazy Kill*, but the lieutenant tops it with a more nonsensical story about two Irishmen.) Blacks directing their violence against one another, when their real oppressors lie elsewhere, strikes Himes as the ultimate irony. But beyond that, such violence describes in physical terms the absurdity of the black situation in America. There is even something funny about it—as if by definition violence somehow defies the laws of nature. "What's funny when a man falls on the ice and seriously hurts himself is to see the limbs flying all ways," he told an English interviewer in 1969. The plethora of violence Himes witnessed as a prisoner would become the informing metaphors, both humorous and grisly, of the absurdist vision of his detective stories many years later.

Although most of Himes's early stories had prison settings, he was apparently influenced at least in part by tough-guy pulp fiction. Among the magazines that reached him in prison, he says, was *Black Mask,* and some of his first pieces probably owe something to *Black Mask*'s prose economy and penchant for flagrant simile.

> He moved down to the other end of the latrine, took three rapid drags from his cigaret. He could feel the smoke way down in the bottom of his lungs. His skin was tight on his face.
> But it was quiet down here. He tried to relax. And then sound creeped into his mind. A broken commode leaked with a monotonous gurgle. The skin crawled on his face like the skin of a snake's belly. ["Crazy in the Stir," 1934]

He was also capable of writing as violent a woman-beating scene as any of his hardboiled contemporaries. In this regard one notes the pulp influence even after his release from prison.

> He never said a word, he just reached around from behind and smacked her in the face with the open palm of his right hand. She drew up short against the blow. Then he hit her under the right breast with a short left jab and chopped three rights into her face when she turned around with the edge of his fist like he was driving nails. ["The Night's for Cryin'," 1937]

Himes says that one of the writers he read as a convict was Chandler, but Chandler's portrayals of Watts Negroes embarrassed him. The pulp writer he obviously admired most was Hammett whose relentless, obsessed criminals foreshadow, in their way, Himes's relentless and obsessed thieves and murderers. The treasures that Himes's and Hammett's crooks seek are lame excuses for the existential pleasure they derive from committing and plotting crimes. Himes may also have borrowed from Hammett the device of having his criminals kill one another off in order to resolve the complications of the plot. Where they differ principally is in their conception of detective heroes.

Precursors of Coffin Ed and Grave Digger appear in "He Knew," a story Himes published in 1933 in *Abbott's Monthly Magazine.* It tells about two middle-aged, tough police detectives, one of whom is called John Jones. (Jones, it will be recalled, is Grave Digger's last name. It is also the last name of the tormented protagonist of Himes's first novel, *If He Hollers Let Him Go.*) In the short story, the cops kill two burglars who turn out to be their

sons. Aside from its O. Henry-like ending and its reverse Oedipal impli-
cations—fathers killing sons—the story embodies the implicitly autobiographical situation of the criminal son writing about the upright fathers of
criminal sons. Insofar as one may say an author identifies with his main
characters, Himes here becomes his own father. Some twenty-six years later
Himes would return to the subject of fathers and their children in his novel,
The Real Cool Killers (1959). Here Coffin Ed discovers that his daughter is
associating with a gang of Harlem delinquents. Although practically all the
other kids in the gang are killed, the life of Coffin Ed's daughter is spared at
the last moment. Perhaps Himes had become somewhat more forgiving.

Himes must have forgotten "He Knew" when he told interviewers in the
1960s that his fictional detective heroes were based on a couple of ruthless
black cops he knew in Los Angeles during World War II. They terrified the
black community with their brutality, he said, and were apparently none too
kind to one another either. One of them, he remembered, killed the other
when he learned he was having an affair with his wife. Himes fused these
real-life cops with the forgotten paternal cops of his early short story to create
his detective heroes. In their dealings with the people of Harlem, Coffin Ed
and Grave Digger emerge as both savage and compassionate, enraged and
decent—the same behavioral extremes Himes attributes to himself in his
autobiographical memoirs.

Another characteristic of Himes's early short stories that anticipates his
subsequent thrillers is his creation of grotesques. In *The Quality of Hurt,*
Himes alludes to Lenny, the gentle but simple-minded murderer in John
Steinbeck's *Of Mice and Men,* who reminds him of some of the convicts he
knew in prison. People not unlike Lenny are found in Himes's fiction of the
1930s but then all but vanish until the first of his detective stories. Each of
the latter contains at least one such creature. They are like nightmare
figures—libidinal, unafraid, and unrestrained. Himes seldom tries to explain
them. He simply describes something of their pasts and then permits them to
run loose. An early version of this type is Pork Chop Smith of "Pork Chop
Paradise" (1938), an ex-con evangelist. Like many of Himes's later criminals, Pork Chop uses religion to exploit the poor and vulnerable. He is
obviously modeled on Harlem's Father Divine, but his ogreish appearance
could just as easily come out of a child's fairy tale. He appears "half frog"
and "half ape" with "huge muscle roped arms and weird long-fingered hands
of enormous size" that "could scratch the calf of either leg. His immense flat
splayed fantastic feet ... grew from abnormally small legs as straight as
sticks." Oddly, he bears a caricatured resemblance to Lillian Taylor's vision
of her husband, Fess, in *The Third Generation.* Mrs. Taylor sees Fess as a
"short, black man with a wiry, simian body [with] bowed legs and pigeon-toed
stance...." Also like Fess, Smith is a marvellously aggressive performer
when black people are about but grins obsequiously in the presence of whites.
It would seem therefore that if Himes transformed his father into a kind of
fictional policeman, he also transformed him into a kind of criminal monster.

On his release from prison in 1936, Himes was paroled in the custody of his mother in Cleveland, but he shortly slipped back into his old ways, associating with gamblers and prostitutes and taking drugs. He later moved in with his father who now lived in Canton and the change improved his prospects. The following year he married Jean Johnson whom he had known before going to prison. He says in his autobiography that he had wanted to marry her earlier but feared his mother's disapproval of her dark skin. Meanwhile he found odd jobs here and there, one as an assistant in a Cleveland library and another as a writer on a WPA state writers' project. But he remained true to his first love—fiction—and continued to write short stories, which now, however, boldly asserted his blackness. Several were of the racial protest variety in the Richard Wright vein and some continued to deal with prison life. In 1939 he moved to Los Angeles seeking steadier income and stayed there through most of the war years. His California output includes a novel that he wrote with the aid of a Rosenwald Fellowship as well as a number of short stories and articles. A few of the latter tell of the black man's faith in the ultimate fulfillment of American democracy—which, in the main, are embarrassing to read today.

Himes says of his California years that they were extremely painful. Racial tensions were high as southern blacks and midwestern and southern whites poured into the state, competing with one another for war jobs and housing. To aggravate the racial potpourri, there was a restless native Mexican-American population and such other minority groups as Filipino- and Japanese-Americans. Race riots were inevitable. Himes describes one in a 1943 article in the National Association for the Advancement of Colored People journal, *Crisis.* He tells how uniformed soldiers and sailors attacked zoot suited Hispanics on the Los Angeles streets and how the Los Angeles police strangely absented themselves during the entire fray. The black protagonist of Himes's first novel makes a terrified allusion to another blatant racial outrage perpetrated by the federal government in 1942 when Japanese-Americans, some of whom had lived in California for generations, were unceremoniously removed from their homes and property to detention camps further east. The action seemed to give implicit sanction to racism. It is of course impossible to measure the exact impact of these events on Himes's writing, but he was becoming increasingly bitter. He believed then and continues to believe now that racism is so endemic to American society that nothing short of well-organized violence can erase it. (One of Himes's projected but never written novels of the 1970s had to do with a race uprising in America in which Coffin Ed and Grave Digger find themselves on opposing sides.) Shortly after the war Himes told Carl Van Vechten that he hoped to expatriate himself.

Himes has related something of his own racial experiences during the 1940s in his memoirs and in interviews. When he arrived in Los Angeles, he sought work as a screen writer, but despite a recommendation by the popular novelist, Louis Bromfield, he had little luck in any of the studios. He tells of overhearing Jack Warner snarl he "didn't want no nigger" on his lot. Himes's other efforts to find steady work were not much happier. In *The Quality of Hurt*, he mentions twenty-three defense jobs he held during the first three years of the war, nearly all of them low-paying despite his skills and intellectual capacities. He was held back, he is convinced, because of his color. The strain affected his marriage, and it is not surprising that the angriest of his novels, *If He Hollers Let Him Go* (1945), was written during these years. Many of the same feral passions that characterize *If He Hollers* reemerge in the last of his fictional works, the crime thriller *Blind Man With a Pistol* (1969), which was also written at a time when racial confrontations were becoming widespread on American city streets.

If He Hollers Let Him Go is a first-person, tension-fraught account by a wartime shipyard worker, Bob Jones, who tells of the racial humiliations he faces day after day. It fuses the genre of protest novel with the violence and style of tough-guy detective stories.

> She was a peroxide blonde with a large-featured, overly made-up face, and she had a large, bright-painted, fleshy mouth, kidney-shaped, thinner in the middle than at the ends. Her big blue babyish eyes were mascaraed like a burlesque queen's and there were tiny wrinkles in their corners and about the flare of her nostrils, calipering down about the edges of her mouth. She looked thirty and well sexed, ripe but not quite rotten. She looked as if she might have worked half those years in a cat house, and if she hadn't she must have given a lot of it away.
>
> We stood there for an instant, our eyes locked, before either of us moved; then she deliberately put on a frightened, wild-eyed look and backed away from me as if she was scared stiff, as if she was a naked virgin and I was King Kong.

Few of Himes's other pre-detective novels adhere so consistently to hard-boiled prose, but they resemble the first in that the lives of his main characters are constantly being threatened.

Yet much of the suspense in these books stems not so much from an external threat to their protagonists' lives as from the protagonists' racial ambivalencè—a fierce anger and envy directed toward whites and the black bourgeoisie, and also, to a certain extent, the black working classes. But even here it is necessary to make qualifications. In *Cast The First Stone* Himes's hero is white and in two of his other novels (*Lonely Crusade* and *The Primitive*) his black heroes have love affairs of sorts with white women. Some of this confusion extends to Himes's attitudes toward the reception of his books. One might think that his rejection of white bourgeois values would make him indifferent to American reviewers. But he is angry because he feels that his books have not enjoyed the critical or commercial success they deserve—and he seems to believe an implicit understanding exists among editors and publishers to keep his books away from readers.

The failure of Himes's first three books to win readers further exacerbated tensions he had been having with his wife, Jean. They lived now mainly in the East—New York City and the New England states—but hard times often kept them apart since one or the other or both had to look for jobs. Around the late 1940s Himes took to extended drinking bouts, and from time to time had affairs with other women. By 1951, he and Jean had parted permanently, and two years later he set sail for France.

In Europe he lived with a married American heiress—in his memoirs he calls her Alva Barneveldt—whom he had met aboard ship and about whom he writes tenderly. They traveled together in France, England, and Spain and Himes wrote the last of his traditional novels, *The Primitive,* dealing with an affair he had once had with a white woman. Alva, who had a husband and children in Holland, eventually went back to the States to stay with her parents, and Himes followed her in 1955. But he was not accorded a very warm reception by his publishers, nor was Alva very sanguine about their future. She "grieved" for her children, she told him, and intended to return to Europe to be with them. There was now not much reason for Himes to remain in the States and so in desperation he took odd jobs to acquire some means to return to France. One of these was as a night porter at a midtown New York Horn and Hardart restaurant that later served as a setting for Himes's only nondetective thriller, *Run Man Run.* More important though, he spent a considerable portion of his leisure time in Harlem where "inadvertently" he "learned so much about the geography of Harlem, the superficiality, the way of life of the sporting class, its underworld, and vice and spoken language, its absurdities" which he would use later in his Harlem detective series. By the end of 1955 he had scraped up enough money to return to Paris.

Himes's subsequent love affairs in Europe and his eventual marriage to an English woman, Leslie Packard, in the late 1960s need not detain us here other than to note that in his memoirs he reveals himself to be often drawn to women who have been badly treated by their husbands and lovers. Alva was such a woman, as is the black novelist's white mistress in *The Primitive.* Himes, of course, knows that he has sometimes behaved badly as a lover, but this has not prevented him from seeking out other women whom he could help, perhaps as expiation. In any case, his detective novels, besides portraying beautiful and dangerous seductresses, also describe vulnerable women who have been cruelly manipulated by men. Himes's treatment of these women is rarely without admiration for their endurance—whether it is the long-suffering blackmailed wife of a rich Harlem gambler (*The Crazy Kill,* 1959), or a murderous narcotics dealer who had been discarded by the pimp she had run away with at the age of fifteen (*The Heat's On,* 1966), or an adolescent Harlem girl who had submitted to whippings by a perverted, middle-aged white man (*The Real Cool Killers,* 1959). What differentiates these women from ordinary damsels in distress is that they seldom accept their fate passively. Himes's exploited women fight back with surprising ferocity—and sometimes succeed.

It was Marcel Duhamel who in late 1956 first advised an impecunious Himes to try writing detective books. Duhamel, long an admirer of Himes, had translated *If He Hollers Let Him Go* into French and was now editor of Gallimard publisher's enormously successful "Série Noire" police novel series. Himes at first demurred. He said he did not know how to write detective books, but Duhamel insisted, suggesting Himes's own life experiences could provide him with sufficient characters and background. Duhamel advised Himes to begin with some dramatic or criminal event in Harlem and then simply allow his imagination free rein. (Himes once told the present writer that he often did not know how his stories would end.) Duhamel also reminded him that his first novel contained terse, tough prose and told Himes to look to Hammett as a model. ("Read Dashiell Hammett. . . . He was the greatest writer who ever lived.") In effect, he recommended the formula: make your story fast-moving and the backgrounds visual and realistic; remember, dialogue is mainly a function of plot; "Keep the suspense going. Don't let your people talk too much. Use the dialogue for narration like Hammett. . . . You keep out of it." The formula worked. Within two weeks Himes returned to Duhamel's office with what turned out to be eighty pages of his first detective novel, *For Love of Imabelle.* Duhamel read it and said he believed it contained enough material for several other novels. He made a few other suggestions, and the following week Himes returned with his book as well as two or three different endings. Duhamel presumably chose the most suitable, and Himes's new career was launched. From here on his detective books would constitute his major fictional output although he would write three other novels—*Pinktoes* (1961), a burlesque of interracial sex and politics in New York; *A Case of Rape* (*Une Affaire de Viol,* 1963, never published in the United States), dealing with American Negroes in France who are accused of killing a white woman; and *Run Man Run* (1966—first published in France in 1959 under the title *Dare-dare*), Himes's non-Harlem thriller which tells of a psychotic white New York cop bent on tracking down and killing an innocent Negro.

Himes says he got the idea for his first detective book from a Paris friend, Walter Coleman, who told him about a confidence game called "the blow." In *Imabelle,* a character is conned into believing that he can duplicate his ten-dollar bills several fold by putting them into a secret steam machine, with unforeseen consequences not only to himself but to a variety of other dubious types who in one way or another get themselves caught up in the con. Some of Himes's other plots stem from memory or from stories he had heard from other friends like Philip Lomax, or the expatriate cartoonist, Ollie Harrington. Another source of inspiration was Faulkner, whose *Sanctuary* and *Light In August* he re-read several times before writing his novels. Faulkner had "an utter influence over my writing," he claims, because he knew how to reproduce the senselessness of American lives, both black and white. "I could lift scenes out of Faulkner and put them down in Harlem and all I had to change was the scene." Six of Himes's eight detective thrillers were printed in five years; three of them were written in a twelve-month period between 1957 and 1958, a period about which he later wrote:

> my mind worked like it was on fire; I could write like a bird sings; I never had to
> hesitate for a word to describe my thoughts, or for a scene to record its
> continuity. [*My Life of Absurdity*]

Himes was never so happy as when he was writing these books. He was not,
after all, writing "art" but popular stuff. "When I went into the detective
field," he told John A. Williams, "I was just imitating all the other detective
story writers." The American detective story, he continued, is "straightforward violence. . . . I just made the faces black, that's all ("My Man
Himes: An Interview with Chester Himes," *Amistad I,* 1970). Himes knew
that he need not worry too much where his plots would lead him. The very
bounds of formula would curb any excess.

Himes knew too that he was addressing primarily a French audience for
whom Harlem was an exotic landscape filled with jungle blacks who were
passionate, violent, and joyous. He could say things to them that he dare not
say at home. He could appear to indulge their fantasies, confirm their pre-
conceptions, and still perhaps instruct them. For if Himes believed he was
writing "straightforward violence," he was also writing in the Afro-American
tradition that aims to tell readers, black and white, the hard truths about black
life. And these truths may sometimes demand something more than a literal
rendering:

> in the murky waters of fetid tenements, a city of black people . . . are convulsed
> in desperate living, like the voracious churning of millions of hungry cannibal
> fish. Blind mouths eating their own guts. Stick in a hand and draw back a nub.
> That is Harlem. [*For Love of Imabelle*]

These books, Himes states, represent a breakthrough because French
readers had hitherto regarded all Negroes as "victims" and thought of
detective stories as the exclusive province of white writers like Simenon,
Peter Cheney, Raymond Chandler and Dashiell Hammett.

At first glance Himes's thrillers appear artless. They are related in the
third person by an omniscient author who shuttles back and forth in time and
locale at will. Plots are bewilderingly interwoven; like Chandler, Himes
places more emphasis on individual scenes than on construction. Often
Coffin Ed and Grave Digger do not appear until the narrative is well
underway and several grotesque crimes have been committed. When they are
called to duty it is sometimes because white police authorities fear bad pub-
licity for Headquarters. A number of very violent confrontations take place
before they succeed in ferreting out their criminals, but the layers and layers
of graft, greed, and betrayal they uncover reveal an incorrigibly corrupt
society.

Like their white predecessors, Coffin Ed and Grave Digger are skeptical
that things can remain clean very long. But whereas white detectives often
blame society's failures on the moral lapses of individuals, Himes's cops vent
their social outrage. Exploitation and racism lie at the very heart of the
system, they say, and the violent and absurd crimes blacks inflict upon one

another are simply a microcosm of what goes on in the larger white world. Their fury mounts with each succeeding book as their author observed from afar the civil-rights struggles on American city streets. Without doubt Himes identified with that anger, but was he also partly furious because now he felt too physically removed? Oddly, one of the characteristics of Himes's later fiction is that the longer he is away from home, the angrier he gets—this at a time, paradoxically, when American racism appeared to be on the wane. Was he now reacting as well to European racism, which he says in his autobiography was not really so very different from what he knew in America?

Himes's Harlem is allegorical, a Hogarthian colony of exploited black people. Many are victims of violence, who themselves shoot, throttle, maul, slice, whip, and stab others. Among their number are hired killers, pimps, addicts, pushers, quacks, prostitutes, crooked cops, numbers racketeers, madams, pederasts, transvestites, and hustlers of all descriptions. They rejoice in such names as Sugartit, Ready Belcher, Uncle Saint, Sister Heavenly, Sweet Prophet, Dummy, Sassafrass, and H. Exodus Clay (an undertaker). Often their physical appearance betrays their monstrous or freakish nature. Consider, for example, Himes's semisardonic, semihumorous description of Sweet Prophet, an enormously successful religious cult figure.

> Sweet Prophet sat on a throne of red roses on a flower-draped float. . . . Over his head was a sun-shade of gold tinsel made in the shape of a halo. . . . His tremendous bulk was impressive in a bright purple robe lined with yellow silk and trimmed with mink. Beneath it he wore a black taffeta suit with white piping and silver buttons. His fingernails, untrimmed since he first claimed to have spoken with God, were more than three inches in length. They curled like strange talons, and were painted different colors. On each finger he wore a diamond ring. His smooth black face with its big buck teeth and popping eyes was ageless; but his long grizzly hair, on which he wore a black silk cap, was snow-white. [*The Big Gold Dream*]

Or Fats, the proprietor of Fats Down Home Restaurant:

> He resembled the balloon that had discovered stratosphere, but hundreds of degrees hotter. He wore an old-fashioned white silk shirt without the collar, fastened about the neck with a diamond-studded collar button, and black alpaca pants; but his legs were so large they seemed joined together, and his pants resembled a funnel-shaped skirt. His round brown head, which could have passed for a safety balloon in case his stomach burst, was clean-shaven. Not a hair showed above his chest—either on his face, nostrils, ears, eyebrows or eyelashes—giving the impression that his whole head had been scalded and scraped like the carcass of a pork. [*The Crazy Kill*]

But Himes's humor is not confined to description. The crimes his characters commit will at times become a kind of grim joke they play on themselves; there is a macabre quality to their violence that one associates with the Keystone Cops or the more sadistic animated cartoons. To illustrate: A motorcyclist in flight from a pursuing police car has his head neatly severed by several sheets of steel that have slipped off the side of a truck. The headless cyclist drives on for a distance before the vehicle crashes (*All Shot Up*, 1960). A sneak thief who has just managed to scissor carefully through the back of a church lady's skirt in order to snip off the money bag that hangs from her waist (while his partner engages her in "holy" conversation) is shortly thereafter hit from the rear by a truck and sent flying through the air like a bird (*Cotton Comes To Harlem*, 1965). A long wicker basket filled with loaves of bread stands in front of a supermarket. A young man lies down on the mattress of bread and is promptly stabbed to death (*The Crazy Kill*, 1959). A crook who is simultaneously trying to kill a goat and crack open a safe accidentally shoots off a half-pint bottle of nitro-glycerine that blows himself up with the goat, the safe, and the entire house (*The Heat's On*, 1965). A bartender leans over the counter and axes off the arm of an unruly knife-wielding customer (*The Real Cool Killers*, 1960). A gunman, Big Six, shuffles through the streets of Harlem with a hunting knife stuck through his head. A woman with two children on their way to see a horror movie shouts at him. "You ought to be ashamed of yourself frightening little children" (*All Shot Up*). At a huge outdoor street revival, presided over by the grotesquely garbed Sweet Prophet, pandemonium breaks loose when a rumor gets out that one of the converts was poisoned drinking the holy water that had been blessed by the Prophet (*The Big Gold Dream*, 1960). And on a less grim note, a tire thief watches his tire sail away from him down the steep decline of Convent Avenue knocking a couple of policemen off their feet (*All Shot Up*).

Himes's humor is verbal as well as physical. He burlesques some of the old-fashioned moral platitudes of the pulp writers. In *For Love of Imabelle*, for instance, a con man who has been passing himself off as a federal agent "apprehends" Jackson, the simple-minded victim of a gang of thieves that has promised to convert his real money into counterfeit money ten times its value. In order to avoid jail, Jackson bribes his captor with money he steals from his boss. Upon receiving the payoff, the marshall admonishes: "Let this be a lesson to you, Jackson. . . . Crime doesn't pay." Himes's humor reflects the hard cynical wit of the urban poor who know how to cheat and lie to the white world to survive physically, and cheat and lie to themselves to survive psychologically. It is this kind of humor that passes in acerbic exchanges between Grave Digger and Coffin Ed as they await criminal payoffs or pay off crooks themselves for information leading to larger prey. Here are Coffin Ed and Grave Digger as they approach one of their information centers, an East Harlem brothel in a filthy tenement.

> "What American slums need is toilets," Coffin Ed said.
> Smelling the odors of cooking, loving, hair frying, dogs farting, cats pissing, boys masturbating, and the stale fumes of stale wine and black tobacco, Grave Digger said, "That wouldn't help much." [*Cotton Comes To Harlem*]

Later when the madam learns of their arrival, she moves toward them "smiling only with her teeth."

> "Hello, boys," she said, shaking hands in turn. "How are you?"
>
> "Fine, Sarah, business is booming; how's your business?" Grave Digger said.
>
> "Booming too, Digger. Only the criminals got money, and all they do with it is buy pussy. You know how it is, runs hand in hand; girls sell when cotton and corn are a drag on the market. What do you boys want?"

Himes's portrayal of Harlemites shows them lying somewhere between open-mouthed gullibility and tough-minded sophistication. Often they exhibit bawdy, earthy qualities mixed with a kind of urban hipness. The following exchange takes place in a diner between a black counterman and a white homosexual who has come looking for a "sissie."

> I know what you want.
> How you know that?
> Just lookin at you.
> Cause I'm white?
> Tain't that. I got the eye.
> You think I'm looking for a girl.
> Chops is your dish.
> Not pork.
> Naw.
> Not overdone.
> Naw. Just right. [*Blind Man With a Pistol*]

The adventures in Himes's Harlem are wild, slapstick, violent, and improbable, but Himes says the improbability of his tales corresponds to a realistic vision of black life in America: "Realism and absurdity are so similar in the lives of American blacks, one cannot tell the difference." Himes does realistically convey the sights, sounds, and smells of Harlem: the extremes of weather, the grey streets and buildings, the loving delights of soul food, the names of taverns, nightclubs, restaurants, the look of alleys, junk shops, butcher shops, bars, gangster pads, brothels, gambling dens, subway stations, furnished rooms, tenement flats, department stores, warehouses, bridges, police stations, and "shooting galleries" where addicts service themselves. But in his 1976 autobiography, Himes says he now thinks of himself not primarily as a realist or as a protest writer, but as an "absurdist"; by revealing blacks absurdly oppressing one another, he was much more of a modernist than he had at first imagined. Although they had begun as nothing more than potboilers, his books have become parables.

Yet if he is an absurdist, he is not without compassion for some of the victims of oppression—whether they have been used by people of their own race or by outsiders. One thinks of the female domestic in *The Big Gold Dream* who stabs her minister, Sweet Prophet, after she learns he wanted her killed. She says she had known all along that he had been trying to steal her money but she remained devoted to him because in her otherwise dreary world she had to believe in someone. Or even more absurdly, there is the giant albino Negro, Pinky, in *The Heat's On,* who kills his father when he learns the latter is planning to emigrate to Africa without him. The father, it seems, feared that African blacks would reject Pinky because he is too light-skinned.

Himes's Harlem remains largely an inner vision, a crazy maze of frustration and evil through which Coffin Ed and Grave Digger must thread their way. To do this, they obviously make their compromises. For them, violence, cupidity, treachery, and brutality are norms of human behavior, and they rarely delude themselves about the true nature of their jobs.

> They took their tribute, like all real cops, from the established underworld catering to the essential needs of the people—gamekeepers, madams, street-walkers, numbers writers, numbers bankers. But they were rough on purse snatchers, muggers, burglars, con men, and all strangers working any racket. And they didn't like rough stuff from anybody else but themselves. "Keep it cool," they warned. "Don't make graves." [*For Love of Imabelle*]

Still, they have their own peculiar code of honor: they are fiercely loyal to one another (indeed their personalities are scarcely distinguishable), and they possess a high-minded zeal to protect the downtrodden poor from their worst exploiters, black and white. But if beneath their rough exteriors they are Lochinvars, they are nonetheless ambivalent about the roles they play. They recognize that the police department that employs them is an extension of the larger society that has brutalized and degraded their community, which may in part explain the excesses of violence they employ on persons (almost always black) whom they suspect of wrongdoing. Are they directing their rage away from themselves for serving an oppressive society? Are they expressing subconscious hostility toward their own people? Must black cops be tougher on blacks than white cops? Or is their brutality really justified? Perhaps because he has been unable to truly answer these questions, and can only rarely even ask them, Himes has been unable to go on with his detective series.

To a degree the reason may lie in the contradictions of the hardboiled detective genre itself. Rather than transcend the formula as Hammett and Chandler would occasionally do, Himes carries the dime detective world view to its logical conclusion in absurdity—tough-guy fiction thereby becoming its own moral, metaphysical, and social comment. For Himes the genre *is* the message with its formula that depends upon unconscious assumptions about existence (violent), human behavior (irrational), sex (dangerous), power (malevolent), and society (corrupt). But, for all that, the genre also implies a modicum of faith in external justice. Despite the isolation of the hero, there must be some recognition somewhere that he has discovered truth and has brought his criminals to their just deserts. If society cannot validate truth and justice, there can no longer be any reason for the detective.

What, after all, is the point of the hero pursuing crooks if no one is to confirm what is delusion and who is evil? For all his sense of being above the law and society, the detective needs law and society not simply to flaunt, but to give support to his values and substance to his identity.

All these contradictions come to a head in Himes's last novel, *Blind Man With A Pistol* (1969), for here he creates a society so corrupt and so venal that it becomes impossible for Coffin Ed and Grave Digger to track down their prey. *Blind Man* begins as his other books do, with Himes introducing us chapter by chapter to his usual gallery of Harlem low life, most of whom become involved with racist white cops as well as their black counterparts, the sour and cynical Coffin Ed and Grave Digger. The latter are required to investigate three major crimes, each of which may be related to the others, but before they are able to solve any of them, they are inexplicably taken off their assignments. The only thing clear about their situation is that their police superiors are obviously bowing to white and black political pressures in order to protect lucrative Harlem rackets.

The complete breakdown of social morality can only lead to chaos, and Himes is especially good at producing chaotic images in his absurd, upside-down Harlem mirror. Somewhere near the middle of the novel Himes describes the convergence from different directions of three parades at 135th Street and Seventh Avenue on Nat Turner Day. Each of the groups represents an opposing ideology: Brotherly Love, Black Power, and Black Jesus. The first, a mob of white and black marchers mindlessly gripping hands, is led by a simple-minded black youth and his dumpy, middle-aged Swedish mistress, while the latter two parades are headed by unprincipled black phoneys. At a critical juncture, all the marchers fling themselves madly on one another whereupon the confusion is compounded by an invasion of police. Himes paints the scene in broad comic strokes but below the surface one senses utter revulsion at the simplistic slogans and cure-alls that aggravate the sicknesses of the black community. Blacks who exploit other blacks do what whites have done to blacks from time immemorial. Only at the very end of the novel does a white/black confrontation take place, but characteristically, it is a confrontation that makes no sense at all. Cops and Negroes shoot it out with one another near a subway station without either knowing why. Meanwhile Coffin Ed and Grave Digger stand idly by shooting at rats fleeing a condemned tenement house.

Did Himes intend the rotting tenement as a metaphor for his country? Do the fleeing rats also bespeak an attitude toward some of Himes's fellow citizens? Whatever the answer, the detective thriller has come to a full stop. Clearly one cannot single out a rat in a house full of rats.

Since the publication of this book Himes, now in his seventies and ailing, appears to have retired from the hurly-burly. No new fiction has emerged since 1969, and he now lives quietly with his English wife in a remote village in Spain.

CHAPTER 5

Ross Macdonald: Gentle Tough Guy

If Chester Himes's black cops are somewhat distant cousins to Dashiell Hammett's Op and Raymond Chandler's Philip Marlowe, Ross Macdonald's Lew Archer is their direct descendant. An astute observer of American popular letters, Macdonald made a decision early in his writing career to produce hardboiled detective stories in the Raymond Chandler mode. The decision was in part motivated by financial need and in part by the desire to discover whether or not modern popular forms could contain and convey Macdonald's mythological and psychoanalytical concerns. As the years passed, Macdonald came to understand that, for him, writing detective fiction was a way of dredging up and confronting a forgotten and bitter youth. Surely no other writer in recent times has been so unabashedly confessional about the autobiographical elements in his works. Indeed so aware is he of their psychoanalytical import that one wonders whether or not his self-consciousness may not in itself conceal something deeper. In any event, Macdonald tells us that he perceives all his fictional characters, good and bad, as aspects of himself. This is especially true of his principal hero, the middle-aged detective, Lew Archer, who in seeking the secrets of others, is perhaps discovering his author's secrets as well. In the course of years, Archer has gradually shed some of his toughness and now comports himself in gentler fashion without a gun. What all this may mean is that Macdonald has learned to forgive himself.

Perhaps we should rejoice that at least one of our popular authors does not associate masculinity with violence. For whatever else he may be, Macdonald is a child of the post-World War II neo-Freudian zeitgeist that has posited that human beings of either sex are composites of so-called masculine and feminine traits. But along with an absence of absolute sexual archetypes, there are corresponding moral equivocations. Good and evil are not so much matters of personal responsibility, as in Chandler, as they are matters relating to social class, family upbringing, and cultural influences. Thus there are few hardened professional criminals in Macdonald's last novels; instead there are unhappy, troubled, and alienated murderers of both sexes whose childhood years had been rent with misunderstanding. It is difficult to hate them—one can only feel sorry for them—and a sympathetic detective like Lew Archer cannot beat them up. His sense of moral ardor has been displaced by psychoanalytical compassion. All of this may sound civilized, but one wonders how, in novels, society as a whole is expected to sustain itself when its sense of right and wrong has been fudged over by psychoanalysis. Macdonald's work challenges one of the main precepts of popular writing, which sees the detective's job as including the making of clear moral choices, even when the alternatives are not clear.

Macdonald, whose real name is Kenneth Millar, was born of Canadian parents near Santa Barbara, California in 1915. When Macdonald was about three the Millar family returned to Canada and shortly thereafter his parents separated. Macdonald is not clear about his father's occupation. At one point he writes he was a sea captain and at another that he was a journalist. His mother, Ann Moyers, had been a nurse. After the separation Kenneth evidently became more his mother's charge, but he tells of being shuttled about between both parents' families for a period extending through his high school years. He says that when he was in high school he once counted to himself fifty rooms that he had lived in. Although his relatives were kind, he writes, these constant moves imbued in him a sense of being an outsider that he never overcame. Despite his Canadian upbringing—or possibly because of it—his mother often reminded him he was an American because he had been born in the United States, and consequently, from his earliest years, he not only longed to return to the land of his birth, but to the place of his birth (California)—an aim he ultimately realized. It is striking how often his novels depict characters, not unlike their author, who as youths drift about from one locale to another, trying to find themselves and their place in the world.

To compound Macdonald's anxieties, the Depression years struck when he was about fifteen, making it more difficult for his relatives to provide for his education. As a result, he yearned, paradoxically, both for upward mobility and for a blessed sense of rootedness, but both dreams were often blighted by poverty. "My childhood," he writes, "was profoundly divided by the rich and the poor, the upright and the downcast, the sheep and the goats. We goats knew the moral pain inflicted not so much by poverty as by the doctrine, still current, that poverty is always deserved." Like the youthful, expatriated Chandler whose survival also depended on the goodwill of relatives, Macdonald tried to regard himself as beyond poverty but seems at the same time to have become sufficiently class conscious to regard both the rich and the middle class with suspicion.

After graduating from high school, he writes, he wanted to go on to college but because he was unable to pay his way, he felt trapped. He says he thought of himself as being "at the same time two radically different kinds of people, a pauper and a member of the middle class." But such a divided sense of social identity really only means he imagined himself classless, which may suggest why the figure of the classless, marginal, hardboiled detective appealed to him as a fictional hero. Certainly Lew Archer's loyalties appear torn between his rich and bourgeois clients and the poor, declassed, and disoriented persons he pursues. Furthermore, many of the young people Archer deals with (aspects of the youthful Macdonald?) express hostility to the adult world because they view all levels of society as grasping and dehumanized. Ordinarily, the hardboiled genre takes a dim view of violators of established social and cultural norms—indeed the tough detective often takes it upon himself to protect or restore these—but Macdonald equivocates. His attacks, as we shall see, often appear as much directed at American values as at those who would transgress them. In any case, no other producer of the popular culture has been so sympathetic to the aims of the "counterculture" of American youth.

If the Depression years engraved psychic scars on the young Millar, there were compensations. At one point, when he was fourteen, he was removed from a high school because his aunt could no longer afford his tuition. At his next school, the Kitchener-Waterloo Collegiate and Vocational School in Ontario, he met his future wife, Margaret Sturm, who would one day become supportive of his literary endeavours. While at Kitchener, Macdonald began producing sketches and parodies for his high school literary magazine. Two of these, "The South Sea Soup Co." (1931), a parody of Sherlock Holmes, and "Philo France in the Zuider Zee" (1932), a parody of S.S. Van Dine's dilettante intellectual detective, Philo Vance, point to a youthful lack of reverence for the genteel detective. Still, all parodies are, in their way, love letters to the works burlesqued, and insofar as Macdonald's later writings depend less and less on violent action and more and more on his detective's mental powers, perhaps the author is moving glacially toward the kind of fiction that once so amused him. This is not to say that Archer has become the old-fashioned gentleman private investigator, but that the pre-Hammett ratiocinative tradition is not totally submerged.

Doubtless other immersions in the popular culture helped prepare the young Millar for his future career. He speaks of reading spy thrillers, boys' magazines and adventure pulps, and, of course, *Black Mask*. He knew and enjoyed Hammett's writings and later in the 1930s came to recognize Chandler as a master. But in addition to the obvious influences, there are two perhaps less apparent—the radio and the movies. As a youngster, Macdonald writes, he loved to go with a favorite uncle to films where part of the program consisted of weekly "serials" in which the hero was left in dire peril at the end of each episode. Dangers resolved the following week led only to new ones, and audiences, especially children, were enticed to return to discover how matters turned out. Radio soap operas and adventure serials followed a similar format. It is a kind of strategy that extends at least as far back as the nineteenth century when Dickens, among others, wrote serialized novels for magazines whose chapters always ended at suspenseful moments. Macdonald's chapters are crafted in like fashion, alternating between resolutions and crises. Certain other characteristics of Macdonald's fiction suggest early media influences. His dialogue resembles the terse sounds and flat rhythms of radio scripts and screenplays rather than the stylized Americanese of Chandler. Even Macdonald's pictorial descriptions correspond in their way to wide sweeps of a camera across a framed landscape. Macdonald writes such scenes usually at the start of a chapter before focusing in on his detective's thoughts, or on his confrontations with other people.

> It was a clear late twilight when the jet dropped down over the Peninsula. The lights of its cities were scattered like a broken necklace along the dark rim of the Bay. At its tip stood San Francisco remote and brilliant as a city of the mind, hawsered to reality by two great bridges—if Marin and Berkeley were reality. [*The Zebra Striped Hearse*]

Shortly after graduating from high school, Macdonald found work as a farmhand, but by 1933 he had evidently saved enough money to enter the University of Western Ontario in London, Ontario. Three years later, in 1936, he took time off to travel and study in Europe and spent two months in Nazi Germany that provided him with material for his first novel. Upon his return to college in 1937 he again met Margaret Sturm whom he had not seen since high school. A courtship ensued, and the day following his graduation in June 1938, they married. That summer they moved to Ann Arbor, Michigan where he enrolled as a graduate student in English literature at the university. But after a few months, they returned to Canada where at the University of Toronto Macdonald took courses that would enable him to teach in Canadian secondary schools. The following year he started a new career as a teacher of English and history at his old high school in Kitchener.

In the interim Margaret had given birth to a daughter and Macdonald, to supplement his income, began to write sketches, verse, and reviews for the Toronto Sunday papers at a penny a word. Between 1939 and 1941 he produced roughly thirty-five of these pieces, but in the latter year he was awarded a full-time teaching fellowship at the University of Michigan (he had been turned down for a similar fellowship at Harvard), and the three Millars now took up permanent residence in the United States.

Macdonald's academic and literary careers would have been a great deal different had it not been for Margaret, who under the name Margaret Millar, became a prolific mystery novelist herself. Her first novel was published in 1941, three years before Macdonald's, who assumed the pseudonym to avoid confusion between them. The five novels she wrote between 1941 and 1944 allowed him to pursue his graduate studies and provided him with inspiration and incentive to write his own books. To his credit, Macdonald has frequently acknowledged his debt. "By going ahead and breaking trail, she helped to make it possible for me to become a novelist, as perhaps her life with me had helped to make it possible for her."

Macdonald's feelings about Margaret may be related to his sympathetic portrayals of women—a rarity in tough guy fiction. Macdonald offers us few of Chandler's seething sexpots or Hammett's pathological liars, although occasional murderesses emerge, whose familial, religious, or puritanical upbringings have distorted their personalities. These creatures seem to be loosely inspired by some of Macdonald's Canadian relatives. But, on the whole, Macdonald's female characters are persevering, intelligent and loyal, and often stronger than their male counterparts.

Macdonald's academic years affect his fiction in several ways. College campuses, students, and professors and their wives appear with increasing frequency in the later novels, beginning with *The Galton Case* (1959); and on a thematic level, many of these books contain allusions to Oedipal quests and mythic adventures that one associates with the symbolic approach to literature particularly favored by English departments during Macdonald's university years. Another source for his fiction lay in Macdonald's studies of the nineteenth-century poet, Samuel Taylor Coleridge. Macdonald became something of a Coleridge specialist during his Michigan years—Coleridge eventually becoming the subject of his doctoral thesis—but even in high school he had shown curiosity about the poet, declaring in his yearbook that he hoped one day to complete Coleridge's unfinished masterpiece about a woman possessed, "Christabel." However jocularly intended, his announcement probably reveals a youthful interest in abnormal psychology which he would put to some use later on in his literary career. But what may have appealed most to Macdonald about Coleridge was the latter's efforts to describe the unnatural and supernatural in realistic terms, for in certain respects Macdonald's detectives would try to do the same thing— cope with the mysterious and inexplicable as if they were concrete realities. Macdonald himself has traced Coleridge's influence on his work to his influence on Poe, the American creator of the detective genre, who in turn influenced Baudelaire, the most prodigious creator of an isolated persona in the "urban inferno." The Baudelarian projection, Macdonald believes, serves in some respects as the psychological model of the private detective from Holmes to Spade to Marlowe.

Yet for all these influences, Macdonald also remains very much a writer of the popular culture. Despite his clear debts to literature of the high art tradition, he has always insisted—if somewhat academically—that popular mystery fiction contains possibilities for great art that critics overlook.

> Its social and psychological range is already immense and I believe this convention could support a full scale philosophical assault on the problem of evil. [*Current Biography*, 1953]

Macdonald seems to be aiming for a middle ground in his fiction where the archetypical narrative is somehow married to the social realism and popular conventions of the hardboiled narrative. As his career unfolds, we find him moving towards the delineation of a hero who also lies somewhere between mainstream fiction's meditators and the "doers" of hardboiled action.

The Macdonalds' move to Michigan in the fall of 1941 preceded by a few months America's entry into World War II. The following year Macdonald received his Master's degree, and shortly thereafter, perhaps remembering his sea captain father, attempted to enlist in the United States Naval Reserve. He was turned down (he does not say why), but evidently tried again because in 1944 he became an ensign. Meanwhile at Michigan he had begun his first novel, a spy thriller of sorts, *The Dark Tunnel,* which drew in part on his reminiscences of Nazi Germany. He worked on this book in the fall of 1943 at night in an office of one of the classroom buildings and says that the terror that permeates the book "was my own . . . at the act of committing myself to a long piece of writing."

Tunnel was published in 1944 while Macdonald was attending Officer Candidate School at Princeton. Margaret and his daughter followed him East and later on took up residences in Boston and San Diego as he moved about from port to port. Some time afterwards, he served as a communications officer on an escort carrier in the Pacific where he apparently found time to write another spy thriller, *Trouble Follows Me.* Like his first book, *Trouble* is about an ordinary citizen who finds himself suddenly sucked into an international intrigue, a dilemma not unlike that of the protagonist of *The Thirty-Nine Steps,* the spy thriller of the Canadian writer, John Buchan, whom Macdonald mentions reading as a young man. *Trouble* was published in 1946, the year of Macdonald's discharge from the Navy. He does not tell what battle action he saw, but in several of his short stories and novels his characters allude to their wartime experiences.

On reentering civilian life, Macdonald joined his wife and daughter, who were now living in Santa Barbara. That same year, 1946, a Macdonald short story, "Find the Woman," appeared in which Lew Archer makes his fictional debut. Although Macdonald has almost without exception produced a book a year since then, Archer did not appear again until 1949, this time as the protagonist in the novel, *The Moving Target.* Each of Macdonald's succeeding works has featured Archer who in his first several books appears closely modeled on Chandler's Philip Marlowe. In 1951 Macdonald received his Ph.D. at the University of Michigan and from then on, to all external appearances, his literary career has been a success both in critical and monetary terms. Eudora Welty, among others, has recently lauded his work, he has won crime and mystery fiction awards both in England and America, and two of his novels have been turned into films. In addition he has done some college teaching, reviewed books for newspapers and journals, and has actively worked for several conservationist organizations. Yet his years in California have not been unalloyed triumphs. Ten years after his return, he writes, "seismic disturbances" occurred in his life that deeply affected his subsequent fiction.

He does not spell out these disturbances, but judging from some of the things he says, it appears that certain childhood anxieties were reignited by fears of failure. "My half-suppressed Canadian youth and childhood rose like a corpse from the bottom of the sea to confront me," he writes. Whether as a consequence or not, in 1956 he moved back to the Bay area of San

Francisco not very far from his birthplace at Los Gatos where he may have undergone psychoanalysis. "There I went through belated mental growing pains trying to understand the peculiar shape of my life." But if he could not change the shape of his life, he decided to "make the best of it," and the following year, 1957, he returned to Santa Barbara where he has lived ever since.

Although Macdonald now feels that he has learned to cope with his past, the yearnings of marginal and alienated youth, poverty, anger, and family failure persist as strong elements in his writings, which may mean that literature remains for him a sublimating process. Often Macdonald's young characters feel something irrevocably lost in their lives which, perhaps like their author, they try desperately to recover. This may be one reason why Macdonald has become so active a conservationist. For him, as we shall see, physical nature and human nature are mysteriously linked, and the neglect and erosion of the one is a sure sign of the depleted condition of the other.

For the purposes of this study, Macdonald's writings may be divided into three parts: his predetective spy and thriller stage (four novels, 1944–1949), his hardboiled stage (six novels, 1949–1959), and his "medium boiled" stage (fourteen novels, 1959–1977). As a medium boiled detective, Lew Archer is compassionate, lonely, and psychologically insightful; often identifying with his clients. The three stages may overlap to some degree (Lew, for example, does reveal a "psychological" predisposition in his first novel), but Macdonald, by his own admission, says Archer did not really shed his Marlowe image until *The Doomsters,* 1958. This study will focus on the more recent portrayal of Archer, for despite the plethora of tough guy detectives who once again inhabit the media, Lew's more moderate ways represent the wave of the future.

To understand the new Archer it is helpful to take into account the changed literary atmosphere of post-World War II America, the period in which Macdonald came of age as an author. Fascism and its attendant evils may have been vanquished, but it was not all that certain that good had triumphed. Recession, fears of nuclear holocaust, the Cold War, the Korean War, social animosities, and periodic searches for "subversives" had contributed to an air of unease. For many writers the clarity with which moral and social issues had once been perceived no longer existed, and the bewildered protagonists of such mainstream novelists as Saul Bellow, James Baldwin, Ralph Ellison, J. D. Salinger, Bernard Malamud, and Flannery O'Connor, among others, seemed to retreat into themselves. They are no longer sure of the "reality" of their worlds nor of the efficacy of social action. As a result they struggle more with the contradictions of their psyches than with the forces of the external environment. Archer shares this immersion in the complexities of the mind. By occasionally conceding his own failings, including latent lust and sadism, and focusing more and more on the psychological deficiencies of his enemies, Archer is in effect saying that he is not so appalled at their "badness." Indeed he attempts to balance his sense of social justice with what he knows about emotional illness. In *The Doomsters* (1958), the novel Macdonald regards as his break with the tenderhearted toughness of the Chandler tradition, Archer manifests much compassion for a male character who mistakenly believes he is responsible for his parents' deaths, and for his wife, the real murderer who has been constantly humiliated, manipulated, and abused by people more powerful than she. At the close of the novel there is some question whether or not Archer believes that she is morally responsible for her crimes.

Psychoanalytically more revealing, Macdonald believes, was *The Galton Case* (1959), published the following year. It tells in part of a young man's semi-exile and return, a theme Macdonald had dealt with in earlier novels. But here, significantly, the young man's outward conformity masks a restless anger, presumably mirroring something of the psychology of the young Millar. The novel is Oedipal in that much of the violence is directed against fathers and father-surrogates. But the reasons for the violence are not necessarily Freudian. According to Macdonald's admittedly private understanding of the Oedipal myth as set out in his preface, Oedipus strikes down his father, not out of ignorance, but because he knows his father had banished him from his home country. This probably corresponds to Macdonald's repressed anger at his own father for having taken him away from his childhood home.

The novel details Archer's search for an elderly heiress's son and grandson. The latter has never been seen by other members of the family because his father, Tony Galton, had been banished some twenty years earlier for marrying beneath his station. Archer determines that the rebellious Tony, who had appropriated the name John Brown, was murdered some time in the mid-1930s, but a youth of twenty turns up who may or may not be his son. While John Brown, Jr. professes to be seeking the home from which he had been taken in infancy, Archer's investigations, like Philip Marlowe's, put him in touch with persons of all social classes, including aging bohemian poets, thugs, and underworld tycoons. Archer's itinerary takes him from his Southern California community to the Bay area of San Francisco, to Las Vegas, and thence to Michigan and Canada; interestingly, in attempting to authenticate young Brown's story, Archer in a general sort of way reverses the route Macdonald himself had taken when he emigrated from Canada. Perhaps in his fashion Macdonald was retracing his own life through Brown.

Brown himself is ultimately revealed as both a charlatan and the real son of Tony Brown, possessing in consequence a divided sense of identity which is probably very like Macdonald's own attitudes about himself during adolescence. In his preface, Macdonald writes that to tell John Brown's story other than through an intermediary like Archer would have been for him too emotional an undertaking. The younger Brown's relentless search for his parents' ancestral home is matched in its way by Archer's obsessive quest for truth. It is as if in endeavoring to find out who Brown is, he is endeavoring to find out something about himself. He is an achingly lonely figure (some years back, we learn in a vague aside, Archer's wife had walked out on him) who falls precipitously in love with a woman Brown had once abandoned. By taking Brown's mistress—however momentarily—Archer changes roles with the pursued, symbolically becoming one with him.

If Archer and Brown resemble one another, young Tom Lemberg, a small-time crook, represents certain aspects of both. Lemberg, Macdonald writes, suggests the coarser side of Brown's nature, but we also remember Archer telling us in *The Doomsters* that as a young man he too had been "a junior-grade hood ... kicking the world in the shins" until a kindly policeman helped reform him. Figures like Brown and Lemberg, Macdonald says, are more interesting and substantive than Archer. The latter, he believes, serves mainly as a sounding board for others, "a consciousness in which the meaning of other lives emerges." But this is not entirely true. There is something confessional in Archer's tone, whatever he is relating, that implicitly describes a complicated emotional life. His sadness is not the sadness of a Philip Marlowe, who perceives himself as a lone paragon of virtue in a sea of evil, but rather the sadness of a man who not only knows his limitations but knows also the secret sorrows of others.

In *The Galton Case*, therefore, Macdonald is at pains to show Archer's "human" side. Not only does he fall in love easily but he is also not very adroit in his handling of the case. He says from the start, for example, that he is convinced he will never be able to track down the heiress's son and grandson, and later when he does meet John Brown, Jr., he cannot make up his mind whether to believe him or not. At one point he practically allows Tom Lemberg to steal his car from under his nose, and at another, he foolishly announces who he is to a band of thugs who easily overcome him. Even his subsequent release is less than glorious. After battering him to a pulp, they express their contempt by simply letting him go. (Contrast this to Ned Beaumont's heroic survival after a similar beating in Hammett's *The Glass Key*.) Finally, Archer himself is not always honorable. Near the end of the novel, he once again confronts Tom Lemberg whose arm is in a sling. But Archer, still angry about Tom's theft of his car, swings hard at the incapacitated youth.

In this book, Archer has not altogether shed his hardboiled ways. When, for instance, he is mistakenly arrested by the police on suspicion of murder, he defies them with wisecracks in much the same manner as Philip Marlowe might have. His style, too, will occasionally sound as if it were lifted from the pulps.

> The houseman came up close to me and smiled. His smile was wild and raw like a dog's grin, and meaningless except that it meant trouble. ... He invited violence as certain other people invite friendship.

More revealing though than Archer's hardboiled style is the very American notion that violence is somehow regenerative. Archer discovers that his brutal beating has reduced him to the helplessness of an infant; at first he can only eat baby food. But he has undergone a kind of death and is now reborn. Perhaps this is one of the ways the later generation of tough guys cope with their peculiarly private fear of death: there are no large moral or societal or cultural consequences to these ritual beatings. That the hero survives is apparently all the spiritual sustenance he will need—until his next beating.

Despite its hardboiled trappings, *The Galton Case* has touches of other literary genres. It is first of all a kind of bourgeois fairy tale. It tells, after all, how John Brown, Jr., an unhappy impecunious dreamy youth, travels thousands of miles to recover his princedom. The rags-to-riches content is, however, adulterated by something gothic as when, for example, the decapitated skeleton of John Brown, Jr.'s father is discovered. Several of Macdonald's other novels also contain disinterred or drowned corpses, signaling that unacknowledged sins and wicked family histories cannot remain forever buried. The sensibility here is as much Aeschylian as it is Oedipal. Finally, Macdonald writes a kind of psychological thriller. The questions Archer asks the various principals in his novels are not unlike the ones a psychiatrist might ask, and he induces much from gestures, facial expressions, and the way people move. Archer's interviews constitute the novel's main actions. Older characters reveal that somewhere in their past they have suppressed fears of sexual inadequacy, hatred, envy, and lust. Because they are emotionally stunted, they fail to communicate with their children who, in turn, flee, to seek new identities.

In his latest adventures, Archer appears less prone to physical danger and ritual beatings than in his earlier Marlowesque years. One reason may be that he now meets fewer professional criminals. The increasing stress on psychological conflict in the later novels comes at the expense of the more easily dramatized class antagonisms that had marked the hardboiled formula. But Macdonald remains loyal to the hardboiled tradition, continuing to shape his adventures to conform to popular conventions, even though Archer no longer acts tough.

In several short autobiographical pieces, Macdonald states almost defensively that he can best cope with the violence of his emotions by submitting them to the discipline of received popular forms. He has accomplished this, he says, by dispersing his ego among a variety of characters, thereby distancing himself from the dangers of excessive subjectivity. He also believes that the detective novel is one of the most accurate gauges we have of our fragmented urban lives.

Macdonald's observations are probably well taken. As we noted in the introductory chapter, one of the functions of the tough detective novel is to uncover the invisible social bonds that tie together overspecialized and atomized societies. By searching the past for "causes" and moving up and down the social hierarchy for solutions, the detective stamps meaning on what otherwise may seen random and arbitrary events. In this fashion the popular culture preempts the diminishing authority of the church, state, or family to give value to human experience. The detective's role corresponds to that of the hero in the nineteenth-century urban novels of Balzac and Dickens. He uncovers the known or unknown links in the fortunes, lives, and activities of people in and out of the reader's immediate experience; by so doing he conveys an overall sense of social, economic, and political relationships. To this extent then, the modern detective story is a descendant of the classic nineteenth-century novel; it tries to imagine a *whole* community— and it does not really matter very much that the community may be evil. What does matter is that certain communal patterns and purposes are given to human actions—which undoubtedly reassures some readers, especially when one considers that most mainstream and elitist novels emphasize and occasionally celebrate human alienation.

Partially the sense of a larger community is satisfied by the private eye's delving into the past, becoming a historian of sorts. In Macdonald's case not only are parents and grandparents investigated, but their lives are frequently related to events of national import. In many Macdonald novels, World War II and the Depression years affect not only those who have lived through them, but their descendants as well. (For example, in *Sleeping Beauty*, a corpse floats in from the sea as a reminder of the evils committed during World War II.) In addition, Macdonald injects historical presence by providing his characters with haunting cultural pasts. There are, for example, genteel Bostonians (now removed to California) who carry about with them ancient airs of Puritan sin and Puritan righteousness. There are also Western characters who have exploited America's natural resources in ways reminiscent of the robber barons. And finally Macdonald's hero, Archer, alludes to himself ironically as the modern equivalent of the eighteenth-century stalker, Natty Bumppo, in James Fenimore Cooper's *Leatherstocking Tales*.

Four novels and six years after *The Galton Case* Macdonald published *The Far Side of the Dollar* which won him an award from the Crime Writers' Association of Great Britain. The middle-aged Archer had by now lost much of his tough veneer. In this novel he is far gentler and seems to have gained the knack of winning the trust and affection of the lonely, dispossessed, and isolated, who in *Dollar* include a light-skinned Negro, a teenage girl, and a fortyish woman warder at a school for delinquent boys. Not only is Archer sympathetic to these lost souls but one gathers that, underneath, he is one of them. At one point he learns that a woman with whom he once had an affair was also once the mistress of a client; Archer keeps telling us he too is a loser.

The novel, like so many of Macdonald's others, deals with Archer's search for an adolescent boy, Tom Hillman, who has disappeared from a private boarding school for disturbed youths. There is some question whether the boy has been kidnapped or has vanished because he is not sure who his "real" parents are. Archer's investigations put him in touch with aspects of his own life that he thought he had forgotten. But in addition to the usual social, Oedipal, and Aeschylian themes, *Dollar* captures something of the flavor of a Dickens novel. The school itself is as oppressive as the one in *Oliver Twist* despite the fact that its inmates are the children of the rich. And there are characters in the novel with Dickensian names: Patch, Mallow, Otto Sipe, Dr. Sponti. In a deeper sense, of course, Macdonald owes something to Dickens's concern with the ways adults treat children. Indeed, one of the novel's themes seems to be that parents should not try to live their lives through their children.

Macdonald's metaphors vividly depict the detritus of civilization, like the once-lavish but now decaying Barcelona Hotel in which Tom was conceived in adultery, or the desolate reform school Archer is about to visit at the beginning of the novel. Interestingly, the latter foreshadows the psychological imprisonment of several characters in the book who deny their past. The prison stands near a "slough" called Laguna Perdida, whose name suggests Archer is on his own Pilgrim's Progress. Countering the images of death are those that depict wildlife under siege. As he drives his car through a light rain Archer sees a blue heron "tiny in the distance [that] stood like a figurine at the edge of the ruffled water." Further on in his narration he will look for the heron again but this time in vain. Concomitantly, Archer looks for characters who want to affirm their lives but, like nature itself, seem to vanish under the onslaughts of greed and fear. Archer speaks as both conservationist and humanist when at the start of his quest for the boy, he remarks of an automobile graveyard he passes that it should be studied "the way they study the ruins and potsherds of civilization. It should provide a clue as to why our civilization is vanishing."

The unseen connections between lives past and present, and the hidden bonds that link pariahs to the more respectable members of society are the subject of Macdonald's best book, *Black Money,* published the following year, 1966. Although the novel breaks no new ground, it happily combines mystery with social comedy. The anxious rich in their country clubs are skillfully interwoven with Las Vegas nightclub tycoons, college professors who worry about their teaching loads and inept, desperate, lower-middle-class social climbers. Although the novel pays homage to certain hardboiled traditions including a Chandler-like disquisition on women—"The easy ones were nearly always trouble"—Macdonald tells a witty, literate story with scatterings of answers to its mystery in a French professor's quiz. This novel probably comes closest to marrying the Dupin-Holmes intellectual tradition to the Sam Spade-Philip Marlowe action brand of detecting. If, as in Macdonald's previous novel, one invites a kind of death by denying the past, in *Black Money* it becomes equally dangerous to attempt to reenact a past that may only exist in fantasy. When the Panamanian Cervantes (who pretends to be a French aristocrat in order to marry the girl of his dreams) quixotically attempts to recreate the past, he—like Fitzgerald's *Gatsby*— comes to a violent end.

Foreshadowing this theme, Archer describes in macabre terms middle-aged members of a country club dancing to the tunes of the 1920s and 1930s.

> Together they gave the impression of a party that had been going on too long, till the music and dancers were as worn as the husks of insects after the spiders had eaten them.

People and institutions become symbols of a past whose promises have been illusory.

In his most recent novels Macdonald shifts from social images to nature as the exposer of an atrophying of civilization. The actions in *The Underground Man* and *Sleeping Beauty* take place respectively against a backdrop of forest fires that threaten to consume an entire town, and an oil slick that is menacing California beaches and destroying sea birds. In *The Blue Hammer* (1976), an immense man-made crater scars the landscape as a result of a mining operation. These images impart a surreal air whose objective correlative describes the slow suicide of community and human psyche. Sometimes in these works an otherwise prosaic landscape is laden with images of dehumanization and death. The flat-roofed stucco houses in a declining middle-class neighborhood face "each other across the street like concrete strong points in a forgotten battlefield." An offshore oil platform looks "like the metal handle of a dagger that has stabbed the world and made it spill black blood." A city lying next to a copper mine seems "to have been drained of energy by the huge wound . . . in its side, the endless suspiration of the smelter. The smoke blew over the city like a great ironic flag." A university that looks in the distance like a "medieval fortress town" sheds its romantic aspect close up where buildings are seen to be merely "half-heartedly modern cubes and oblongs and slabs."

At one point, a group of lost and loveless middle-class children stand on the ramshackle porch of their commune and sing songs about "Armageddon and the end of the world" which makes Archer "think of passengers singing hymns on a sinking ship." At the dead of night they look to him like the residue of an apocalypse. And although Archer obviously rejects their credo, he clearly understands their despair. He knows that it is too late for him to reach them, although they in their way have reached him. But there are other young people he may save, perhaps because in part he identifies with them, perhaps because in part he is as confused as they. In *Blue Hammer* he writes:

> My chosen study was other men, hunted men in rented rooms, aging boys clutching at manhood before night fell and they grew suddenly old. If you were the therapist, how could you need therapy? If you were the hunter, you couldn't be hunted. Or could you?

Archer is both hunter and hunted. A cult leader in *The Blue Hammer* says to him, "You seem to be a man engaged in an endless battle, an endless search. Has it ever occurred to you that the search may be for yourself?" In spite of himself, Archer has to admit there may be something to that.

But if Archer is searching for himself, he is nonetheless rescuing the weak and the lost in the process, and in this regard he is not unlike Chandler's knight errant, Philip Marlowe, who perceives his life in similar terms. Archer's adventures take place in a wry and ironic fairy tale world. The Sleeping Beauty whom Archer tries to rescue takes sleeping pills and accuses her selfless protector of being a lecher. But Archer does in fact rescue her and his quest is oddly Arthurian in nature: one of Archer's stops on his journey to find the girl is, for example, called Excalibur Arms. And in *The Blue Hammer,* Archer rescues another damsel in distress whom he finds naked, tied hand and foot, and menaced by an ogrelike killer.

In this work, Archer—never fully selfless—has fallen in love again. It is just possible that like the later Marlowe he may form some kind of lasting relationship. Should this happen, it is no calamity. It may simply mean that the world is getting too tough for one tough guy to handle alone.

CHAPTER 6

Conclusion

Which way did he go?

The tough-guy detective has traveled a considerable distance from Sam Spade's proud amorality to Lew Archer's compassionate identification with both criminal and victim. In between we have seen Chandler's highly moral Marlowe and Chester Himes's despairing Coffin Ed Johnson and Grave Digger Jones. Despite their differences, all of them share a form of self-definition by pursuing evildoers. In the process of defining themselves, they also define their authors and readers, for whatever else they are, popular heroes are creatures of their cultures whose main mission is to reaffirm widespread beliefs and values. No popular author can *overtly* diverge very far from what his readers already believe and want to continue to believe.

Still, one is left wondering whether or not this is what our authors really wanted. In their secret hearts, did they despise formula fiction? Did they—their protestations to the contrary—aspire to write the "great American novel"? There are hints here and there of defiance and unease, but there is also ample evidence that they experienced a kind of freedom and joy in knowing the limits to which they could stretch formula. For just as our authors' works are sometimes mixtures of the trite and the surprising, so too probably were their motives.

All of them, as we have seen, began writing mystery fiction out of economic distress rather than artistic ambition. But to assume popular writers are calculating materialists would be to overlook much of the passion and high spirits of their writing. Obviously they respond to the temper of their times and like so many other Americans they both disbelieve and believe in what their country stands for. While their heroes cling to notions of the sanctity of the individual and the capabilities of ordinary people they often express contempt for official authority and social institutions. And if they are not exactly anti-intellectual, they are certainly suspicious of what may be described as high culture.

Yet despite these propensities, they are themselves often speculative, and eager to understand the present in terms of the past. In *Mumbo Jumbo*

(1972), a parody of the detective novel, the Afro-American author Ishmael Reed, a fervent admirer of Chester Himes, invents a historical past in order to uncover the sources of present-day racism. Although Reed is by no means a tough-guy writer, his novel does suggest some adventurous possibilities for future action detectives. When we look at the personal lives of the authors treated in this book, we note some common attributes. Each felt estranged from or hostile to his father, each had a mobile or rootless childhood, and each felt himself—not without justification—an outsider in his community. Hammett, Chandler and Himes were heavy drinkers, and Chandler and Himes both lived for many years outside the United States. Still, one could draw up similar case histories for any number of traditional and elitist authors—or nonauthors, for that matter. Perhaps the safest thing we can say is that the personal and psychological traits of the authors have some bearing on their heroes' direction.

The tough private eye probably enjoyed his greatest prestige during the 1930s. It may seem odd that the Depression years spawned so many fictional detective heroes, but it may well be that the very failure of American capitalism and the concomitant growth of big government gave rise to the private eye's popularity. The detective was, after all, in business for himself, responsible for his own destiny, and not dependent on the large, impersonal bureaucracies of corporations or the state for his survival. Indeed he defied them. He was, moreover, proving individual effort and enterprise could make a difference. He made sense of a bewildering society as he criss-crossed class lines clearing things up. He was a conservative rebel—an ordinary fellow and celebrant of the Protestant ethic inveighing against the corruption of the rich and powerful and the subversion of traditional values. Finally he was a catcher of crooks, and crime—unlike the mysteries of the economy—was something readers could grasp. There were simply good guys and bad, and the bad needed to be caught. Interestingly, these were the years the newly enhanced FBI also enjoyed its greatest popularity—announcing public enemies and then proceeding to catch them.

Although the fictional private eye's fortunes declined after the Depression years, he still has his readers. Indeed private detective fiction has seen a resurgence in the 1970s after a dip in popularity in the turbulent 1960s. One reason, as we have indicated elsewhere, is that the fictional detective needs a relatively stable social order, however disagreeable, in which to operate. Several of the newer writers evidently see some kind of social equilibrium being restored. (Himes's cops, on the other hand, finally had to give up in racially torn Harlem.)

But if the newer generation of detectives are more optimistic, several of them appear less independent because they now work closely with the police. Although they have superior resources with which to conduct their investigations, they do not make the same kind of moral and social judgments as outsider, classless, private detectives do. Yet the fact that some continue to act on their own and take responsibility for their actions suggests that

American individualism is far from dead—at least in fantasy. That these heroes are also more spread out geographically (as, for instance, Robert B. Parker's Spenser, a Boston detective, or Jonathan Valin's Harry Stoner, a Cincinnati private eye) attests to a readership that still enjoys local color. As a general rule, they are not so murderous as their literary ancestors, nor do they seem to undergo so many vicious beatings. The new breed also appears to hold kinder views about sexually active women. Lastly, they represent a somewhat wider ethnic variety, which may mean that if the melting pot is not melting, the blood ancestory of detectives is not so important a factor in determining their fitness as heroes.

Where will the tough guy go? The answer depends to a large degree on the direction of American culture. Hardboiled detectives, like other popular heroes, exist in part because of the perceived failures of American society to deal justly with crime and other social inequities. But they also represent the ancient American belief that the individual, and not society, is morally responsible for his actions and that he can and should be able to take care of himself, as well as to lend support to the weak and the helpless. Thus critics of both the political left and right who claim the private eye as their own do so with some justification. And since it looks as if American society will remain bureaucratized, unfair, and complicated for a long time to come, it is not unlikely that the detective or someone like him will be around to make life less arduous. His anger and his violence will remain to some degree a measure of his author's and readers' responses to their worlds. No one can tell with certainty the length of his stay, but judging from what we know of the present, there remains a great deal for him to do.

Bibliography

The following lists cite only first editions or first appearances of novels published in the United States. With the exception of Hammett, I have omitted collections of short stories since these frequently vary and are often in and out of print. The reader may, however, consult "Sources and Acknowledgments" for bibliographies citing short-story collections. I have included the last two published anthologies of Hammett's short fiction because their introductions by Lillian Hellman and Steven Marcus are important and because I believe the paper-bound editions of both books are likely to remain in print for some time to come.

Dashiell Hammett

Red Harvest. New York: Alfred A. Knopf, 1929.
The Dain Curse. New York: Alfred A. Knopf, 1929.
The Maltese Falcon. New York: Alfred A. Knopf, 1930.
The Glass Key. New York: Alfred A. Knopf, 1931.
The Thin Man. New York: Alfred A. Knopf, 1934.
The Big Knockover, Selected Stories and Short Novels, Edited and with an introduction by Lillian Hellman. New York: Random House, 1966. Reprinted in Vintage Books Edition, 1972.
The Continental Op, Edited and with an introduction by Steven Marcus. New York: Vintage Books, 1974. Reprinted in Vintage Books Edition, 1975.

Raymond Chandler

The Big Sleep. New York: Alfred A. Knopf, 1939.
Farewell My Lovely. New York: Alfred A. Knopf, 1940.
The High Window. New York: Alfred A. Knopf, 1942.
The Lady in the Lake. New York: Alfred A. Knopf, 1943.
The Little Sister. Boston: Houghton Mifflin Company, 1949.
The Long Goodbye. Boston: Houghton Mifflin Company, 1954.
Playback. Boston: Houghton Mifflin Company, 1958.

Chester Himes

For Love of Imabelle. Greenwich, Conn.: Fawcett, 1957. Reprinted as *A
    Rage In Harlem*. New York: Avon Books, 1965.
The Crazy Kill. New York: Avon Books, 1959.
The Real Cool Killers. New York: Avon Books, 1959.
All Shot Up. New York: Avon Books, 1960.
Cotton Comes to Harlem. New York: G. P. Putnam's Sons, 1965.
Run Man Run. New York: G. P. Putnam's Sons, 1966.
The Heat's On. New York: G. P. Putnam's Sons, 1966.
Blind Man With A Pistol. New York: William Morrow, 1969. Reprinted as
    Hot Day, Hot Night. New York: Dell, 1976.

Ross Macdonald*

The Dark Tunnel. New York: Dodd, Mead & Co., 1944.
Trouble Follows Me. New York: Dodd, Mead & Co., 1946.
Blue City. New York: Alfred A. Knopf, 1947.
The Three Roads. New York: Alfred A. Knopf, 1948.
The Moving Target. New York: Alfred A. Knopf, 1949.
The Drowning Pool. New York: Alfred A. Knopf, 1950
The Way Some People Die. New York: Alfred A. Knopf, 1951.
The Ivory Grin. New York: Alfred A. Knopf, 1952
Meet Me At The Morgue. New York: Alfred A. Knopf, 1953.
Find A Victim. New York: Alfred A. Knopf, 1954.
The Barbarous Coast. New York: Alfred A. Knopf, 1956.
The Doomsters. New York: Alfred A. Knopf, 1958.
The Galton Case. New York: Alfred A. Knopf, 1959.
The Ferguson Affair. New York: Alfred A. Knopf, 1960.
The Wycherly Woman. New York: Alfred A. Knopf, 1961.
The Zebra-Striped Hearse. New York: Alfred A. Knopf, 1962.
The Chill. New York: Alfred A. Knopf, 1964.
The Far Side Of the Dollar. New York: Alfred A. Knopf, 1965.
Black Money. New York: Alfred A. Knopf, 1966.
The Instant Enemy. New York: Alfred A. Knopf, 1968.
The Goodbye Look. New York: Alfred A. Knopf, 1969.
The Underground Man. New York: Alfred A. Knopf, 1971.
Sleeping Beauty. New York: Alfred A. Knopf, 1973.
The Blue Hammer. New York: Alfred A. Knopf, 1976.

*Macdonald has employed several names as author of his books. He uses his real name, Kenneth
Millar, for his first four novels. The author of his fifth novel, *The Moving Target*, 1949, is called
John Macdonald. His sixth through tenth novels are written by John Ross Macdonald.
Beginning with his eleventh novel, *The Barbarous Coast*, 1956, he has been using the name
Ross Macdonald.

Index

About the Author

Edward Margolies is a professor of English and American Studies at the College of Staten Island of the City University of New York. He received his B.A. from Brown University and his M.A. and Ph.D. from New York University. Professor Margolies was Senior Fulbright Lecturer at the University of Nijmegen, Holland in 1977 and Visiting Professor of American Studies at the University of Paris (III), France in 1979. He is the author of *Native Sons—A Critical Study of Twentieth Century Negro American Authors* (Lippincott, 1968), *The Art of Richard Wright* (Southern Illinois University Press, 1969), *A Native Sons Reader* (Editor, Lippincott, 1970), *Afro-American Fiction, 1853–1976* (co-author, Gale Research Co., 1979), and many articles on American literature. Margolies lives in New York City.